— The —
Constitution of the United States of America

John T. Colby Jr.
Publisher

Brick Tower Press
Habent Sua Fata Libelli

THE CONSTITUTION OF THE UNITED STATES OF AMERICA

Brick Tower Press
Manhanset House
Dering Harbor, New York 11965-0342
bricktower@aol.com • www.BrickTowerPress.com

Library of Congress Cataloging-in-Publication Data
The Constitution of the United States of America

I. United States—Constitutional Law.
2. United States—Constitution. I. Colby, John Jr.

ISBN 978-1-883283-80-3, Hardcover
ISBN 978-1-883283-00-1, Trade Paper

Table of Contents

Plato's Apology of Socrates

"I also say the following to these same ones. Perhaps you suppose, men of Athens, that I have been convicted because I was at a loss for the sort of speeches that would have persuaded you, if I had supposed that I should do and say anything at all to escape the penalty. Far from it. Rather, I have been convicted because I was at a loss, not however for speeches, but for daring and shamelessness and willingness to say the sorts of things to you that you would have been most pleased to hear: me wailing and lamenting, and doing and saying many other things unworthy of me, as I affirm—such things as you have been accustomed to hear from others. But neither did I then suppose that I should do anything unsuitable to a free man because of the danger, nor do I now regret that I made my defense speech like this: I Much prefer to die having made my defense speech in this way than to live in that way."

Preface

by John T. Colby Jr.

This edition of the U.S. Constitution presents compelling examples of how the Constitution has served the test of time since it adoption in 1787. Fundamental features of human nature may sometimes conspire to corrupt the intent and understanding the writers established to secure the future of the United States, but basic principles of decency will prevail when applied within its context.

We will update this periodically adding what past generations have referred to as "profiles in courage," as this work is not meant to be overbearing or complex. Our intent is to show the U.S. Constitution in action defending the liberty and freedom this country has long established and fought for.

We establish the J. Boylston Award for Rhetorical Courage as recognition for defending the Constitution of the United States and the principles, beliefs, and common decency everyone deserves.

Susan Margaret Collins is an American politician serving as the senior United States Senator for Maine, a seat to which she was first elected in 1996. A Republican, Collins is the chair of the Senate Special Committee on Aging and is a former chair of the Senate Committee on Homeland Security and Governmental Affairs.

Advise & Consent

Mr. President, the five previous times that I've come to the floor to explain my vote on the nomination of a justice to the United States Supreme Court, I have begun my floor remarks explaining my decision with a recognition of the solemn nature and the importance of the occasion. But today we have come to the conclusion of a confirmation process that has become so dysfunctional, it looks more like a caricature of a gutter-level political campaign than a solemn occasion.

The president nominated Brett Kavanaugh on July 9. Within moments of that announcement, special interest groups raced to be the first to oppose him, including one organization that didn't even bother to fill in the judge's name on its pre-written press release. They simply wrote that they opposed Donald Trump's nomination of "XX" to the Supreme Court of the United States. A number of senators joined the race to announce their opposition, but they were beaten to the punch by one of our colleagues who actually announced opposition before the nominee's identity was even known.

Since that time, we have seen special interest groups whip their followers into a frenzy by spreading misrepresentations and outright falsehoods about Judge Kavanaugh's judicial record. Over-the-top rhetoric and distortions of his record and testimony at his first hearing produced short-lived headlines, which although debunked hours later, continued to live on and be spread through social media. Interest groups have also spent an unprecedented amount of dark money opposing this nomination. Our Supreme Court confirmation process has been in steady decline for more than 30 years.

One can only hope that the Kavanaugh nomination is where the process has finally hit rock bottom. Against this backdrop, it is up to each individual senator to decide what the Constitution's advice and consent duty means. Informed by Alexander Hamilton's *Federalist 76*, I have interpreted this to mean that the president has broad discretion to consider a nominee's philosophy, whereas my duty as a senator is to focus on the nominee's qualifications as long as that nominee's philosophy is within the mainstream of judicial thought.

I have always opposed litmus tests for judicial nominees with respect to their personal views or politics, but I fully expect them to be able to put aside any and all personal preferences in deciding the cases that come before them. I've never considered the president's identity or party when evaluating Supreme Court nominations. As a result, I voted in favor of Justices Roberts and Alito, who were nominated by President Bush. Justices Sotomayor and Kagan, who were nominated by President Obama. And Justice Gorsuch, who was nominated by President Trump.

So I began my evaluation of Judge Kavanaugh's nomination by reviewing his 12-year record on the DC Circuit Court of Appeals, including his more than 300 opinions and his many speeches and law review articles. Nineteen attorneys, including lawyers from the nonpartisan congressional research service, briefed me many times each week and assisted me in evaluating the Judge's extensive record. I met with Judge Kavanaugh for more than two hours in my office. I listened carefully to the testimony at the committee hearings. I spoke with people who knew him personally, such as Condoleezza Rice and many others. And I talked with Judge Kavanaugh a second time by phone for another hour to ask him very specific additional questions. I also have met with thousands of my constituents, both advocates and many opponents, regarding Judge Kavanaugh.

One concern that I frequently heard was that the judge would be likely to eliminate the Affordable Care Act's vital protections for people with preexisting conditions. I disagree with this. In a dissent in Seven-Sky v. Holder, Judge Kavanaugh rejected a challenge to the ACA on narrow procedural grounds, preserving the law in full. Many experts have said that his dissent informed Justice Roberts's opinion upholding the ACA at the Supreme Court.

Furthermore, Judge Kavanaugh's approach toward the doctrine of sever-ability is narrow. When a part of a statute is challenged on constitutional grounds, he has argued for severing the invalid clause as surgically as possible while allowing the overall law to remain intact.

This was his approach in a case that involved a challenge to the structure of the consumer financial protection bureau. In his dissent, Judge Kavanaugh argued for "severing any problematic portions while leaving the remainder intact." Given the current challenges to the ACA proponents, including myself, of protections for people with preexisting conditions should want a justice who would take just this kind of approach.

Another assertion that I have heard often that Judge Kavanaugh cannot be trusted if a case involving alleged wrongdoing by the president were to come before the court. The basis for this argument seems to be two-fold.

First, Judge Kavanaugh has written that he believes that Congress should enact legislation to protect presidents from criminal prosecution or civil liability while in office. Mr. President, I believe opponents missed the mark on this issue. The fact that judge Kavanaugh offered this legislative proposal suggests that he believes that the president does not have such protection currently.

Second, there are some who argue that given the current special counsel investigation, President Trump should not even be allowed to nominate a justice. That argument ignores our recent history. President Clinton in 1993 nominated Justice Ginsburg after the Whitewater investigation was already underway, and she was confirmed 96 to 3. The next year, just three months after independent counsel Robert Fisk was named to lead the Whitewater investigation, President Clinton nominated Justice Breyer. He was confirmed 87 to 9.

Supreme Court justices have not hesitated to rule against the presidents who have nominated them. Perhaps most notably in *The United States vs. Nixon*, three Nixon appointees who heard the case joined the unanimous opinion against him. Judge Kavanaugh has been unequivocal in his belief that no president is above the law. He has stated that *Marbury vs. Madison*, *Youngstown Steel vs. Sawyer* and *The United States vs. Nixon* are three of the greatest Supreme Court cases in history. What do they have in common? Each of them is a case where Congress served as a check on presidential power.

And I would note that the fourth case that Judge Kavanaugh has pointed to as the greatest in history was *Brown vs. The Board of Education*. One Kavanaugh decision illustrates the point about the check on presidential power directly. He wrote the opinion in *Hamdan vs. The*

United States, a case that challenges the Bush administration's military commission prosecution of an associate of Osama bin Laden. This conviction was very important to the Bush administration, but Judge Kavanaugh, who had been appointed to the DC Circuit by President Bush and had worked in President Bush's White House, ruled that the conviction was unlawful. As he explained during the hearing, "we don't make decisions based on who people are or their policy preferences or the moment. We base decisions on the law."

Others I've met with have expressed concerns that Justice Kennedy's retirement threatens the right of same-sex couples to marry. Yet, Judge Kavanaugh described the *Obergefell* decision, which legalized same-gender marriages, as an important landmark precedent. He also cited Justice Kennedy's recent masterpiece cake shop opinion for the court's majority stating that "the days of treating gay and lesbian Americans, or gay and lesbian couples as second-class citizens who are inferior in dignity and worth are over in the Supreme Court."

Others have suggested that the judge holds extreme views on birth control. In one case Judge Kavanaugh incurred the disfavor of both sides of the political spectrum for seeking to ensure the availability of contraceptive services for women while minimizing the involvement of employers with religious objections. Although his critics frequently overlook this point, Judge Kavanaugh's dissent rejected arguments that the government did not have a compelling interest in facilitating access to contraception. In fact, he wrote that the Supreme Court precedent strongly suggested that there was a compelling interest in facilitating access to birth control.

There has also been considerable focus on the future of abortion rights based on the concern that Judge Kavanaugh would seek to overturn *Roe v. Wade*. Protecting this right is important to me. To my knowledge, Judge Kavanaugh is the first Supreme Court nominee to express the view that precedent is not merely a practice and tradition, but rooted in Article 3 of our Constitution itself. He believes that precedent is not just a judicial policy, it is constitutionally dictated to pay attention and pay heed to rules of precedent. In other words, precedent isn't a goal or an aspiration. It is a constitutional tenet that has to be followed except in the most extraordinary circumstances.

The judge further explained that precedent provides stability, predictability, reliance and fairness. There are, of course, rare and extraordinary times where the Supreme Court would rightly overturn a precedent. The most famous example was when the Supreme Court in *Brown vs. The Board of Education* overruled *Plessy vs. Ferguson*, correcting a "grievously wrong decision" to use the judge's term, allowing racial inequality. But someone who believes that the importance of precedent has been rooted in the Constitution would follow long-established precedent except in those rare circumstances where a decision is grievously wrong or deeply inconsistent with the law. Those are Judge Kavanaugh's phrases.

As the judge asserted to me, a long-established precedent is not something to be trimmed, narrowed, discarded, or overlooked. Its roots in the Constitution give the concept of stare decisis greater weight simply because a judge might want to on a whim. In short, his views on honoring precedent would preclude attempts to do by stealth that which one has committed not to do overtly.

Noting that *Roe v. Wade* was decided 45 years ago and reaffirmed 19 years later in *Planned Parenthood vs. Casey*, I asked Judge Kavanaugh whether the passage of time is relevant to following precedent. He said decisions become part of our legal framework with the passage of time and that honoring precedent is essential to maintaining public confidence. Our discussion then turned to the right of privacy on which the Supreme Court relied in *Griswold vs. Connecticut*, a case that struck down a law banning the use and sale of contraceptions. *Griswold* established the legal foundation that led to *Roe* eight years later. In describing *Griswold* as settled law, Judge Kavanaugh observed that it was the correct application of two famous cases from the 1920's, Meyer and Pierce that are not seriously challenged by anyone today.

Finally, in his testimony, he noted repeatedly that *Roe* had been upheld by *Planned Parenthood vs. Casey*, describing it as a precedent. When I asked him would it be sufficient to overturn a long-established precedent if five current justices believed that it was wrongly decided, he emphatically said "no."

Opponents frequently cite then-candidate Donald Trump's campaign pledge to nominate only judges who would overturn *Roe*. The Republican platform for all presidential campaigns has included this pledge since at least 1980. During this time Republican presidents have appointed Justices O'Connor, Souter and Kennedy to the Supreme Court. These are the very three Republican president appointed justices who authored the *Casey* decision which reaffirmed *Roe*.

Furthermore, pro-choice groups vigorously oppose each of these justice's nominations. Incredibly, they even circulated buttons with the slogan "Stop Souter or women will die." Just two years later Justice Souter coauthored the *Casey* opinion reaffirming a woman's right to choose. Suffice it to say, prominent advocacy organizations have been wrong.

These same interest groups have speculated that Judge Kavanaugh was selected to do the bidding of conservative ideologues despite his record of judicial Independence. I asked the judge point-blank whether he had made any commitments or pledges to anyone at the White House, to the Federalist Society, to any outside group on how he would decide cases. He unequivocally assured me that he had not.

Judge Kavanaugh has received rave reviews for his 12-year track record as a judge, including for his judicial temperament. The American Bar Association gave him its highest possible rating. Its standing committee on the federal judiciary conducted an extraordinarily thorough assessment, soliciting input from almost 500 people, including his judicial colleagues. The ABA concluded that his integrity, judicial temperament and professional competence met the highest standards.

Lisa Blatt, who has argued more cases before the Supreme Court than any other woman in history, testified, "By any objective measure, Judge Kavanaugh is clearly qualified to serve on the Supreme Court. His opinions are invariably thoughtful and fair." Ms. Blatt, who clerked for and is an ardent admirer of Justice Ginsburg and who is, in her own words, an unapologetic defender of a woman's right to choose, says that Judge Kavanaugh fits within the mainstream of legal thought. She also observed that Judge Kavanaugh is remarkably committed to promoting women in the legal profession.

That Judge Kavanaugh is more of a centrist than some of his critics maintain is reflected in the fact that he and Chief Judge Merrick Garland voted the same way in 93 percent of the cases that they heard together. Indeed, Chief Judge Garland joined in more than 96 percent of the majority opinions authored by Judge Kavanaugh, dissenting only once.

Despite all this, after weeks of reviewing Judge Kavanaugh's record and listening record and listening to 32 hours of his testimony, the Senate's advice and consent was thrown into a tailspin following the allegations of sexual assault by Professor Christine Blasey Ford. The confirmation process now involved evaluating whether or not Judge Kavanaugh committed sexual assault and lied about it to the Judiciary Committee.

Some argue that because this is a lifetime appointment to our highest court, the public interest requires that it be resolved against the nominee. Others see the public interest as embodied in our long-established tradition of affording to those accused of misconduct a presumption of innocence or in cases in which the facts are unclear, they would argue that the question should be resolved in favor of the nominee.

Mr. President, I understand both viewpoints. And this debate is complicated further by the fact that the Senate confirmation process is not a trial. But certain fundamentally legal principles about due process, the presumption of innocence, and fairness do bear on my thinking, and I cannot abandon them. In evaluating any given claim of misconduct we will be ill served in the long republic if we abandon the presumption of innocence and fairness tempting though it may be.

We must always remember that it is when passions are most inflamed that fairness is most in jeopardy. The presumption of innocence is relevant to the advice and consent function when an accusation departs from a nominees otherwise exemplary record. I worry that departing from this presumption could a lead to a lack of public faith in the judiciary and would be hugely damaging to the confirmation process moving forward.

Some of the allegations levied against Judge Kavanaugh illustrate why the presumption of innocence is so important. I am thinking in particular not at the allegations raised by professor Ford, but of the allegations that when he was a teenager Judge Kavanaugh drugged multiple girls and used their weakened state to facility gang rape.

This outlandish allegation was put forth without any credible supporting evidence and simply parroted public statements of others. That's such an allegation can find its way into the Supreme Court confirmation process is a stark reminder about why the presumption of innocence is so ingrained in our a American consciousness.

Mr. President, I listened carefully to Christine Blasey Ford's testimony before the Judiciary Committee. I found her testimony to be sincere, painful, and compelling. I believe that she is a survivor of a sexual assault and that this trauma has upended her life.

Nevertheless, the four witnesses she named could not corroborate any of the events of that evening gathering where she says the assault occurred. None of the individuals Prof. Ford says were at the party has any recollection at all of that night. Judge Kavanaugh forcefully denied the allegations under penalty of perjury. Mark Judge denied under penalty of felony that he had witnessed an assault. P.J. Smith, another person allegedly at the party, denied that he was there under penalty of felony. Professor Ford's lifelong friend, Leland Kaiser, indicated that under penalty of felony she does not remember that party. And Ms. Kaiser went further. She indicated that not only does she not remember a night like that, but also that she does not even know Brett Kavanaugh.

In addition to the lack of corroborating evidence we also learn facts that have raised more questions. For instance, since these allegations have become public, Prof. Ford testified that not a single person has contacted her to say I was at the party that night.

Furthermore the professor testified that although she does not remember how she got home that evening, she knew that because of the distance she would have needed a ride. Yet, not a single person has come forward to say that they were the ones who drove her home or were in the car with her that night.

And Prof. Ford also indicated that even though she left that small gathering of six or so people abruptly, and without saying goodbye, and distraught, none of them called her the next day or ever to ask why she left. "Is she okay?" Not even her closest friend, Ms. Kaiser.

Mr. President, the Constitution does not provide guidance on how we are supposed to evaluate these competing claims. It leaves that decision up to each senator. This is not a criminal trial, and I do not believe that claims such as these need to be proved beyond a reasonable doubt, nevertheless fairness of this terrible problem.

I have been alarmed and disturbed, however, by some who have suggested that unless Judge Kavanaugh's nomination is rejected, the Senate is somehow condoning sexual assault. Nothing could be further from the truth. Every person, man or woman, who makes a charge of sexual assault deserves to be heard and treated with respect. The #MeToo movement is real. It matters. It is needed. And it is long overdue.

We know that rape and sexual assault are less likely to be reported to the police than other forms of assault. On average, an estimated

211,000 rapes and sexual assaults go unreported every year. We must listen to survivors, and every day we must seek to stop the criminal behavior that has hurt so many. We owe this to ourselves, our children, and generations to come.

Since the hearing, I have listened to many survivors of sexual assault. Many were total strangers who told me their heart-wrenching stories for the first time in their lives. Some were friends that I had known for decades. Yet with the exception of one woman who had confided in me years ago, I had no idea that they had been the victims of sexual attacks. I am grateful for their courage and their willingness to come forward and I hope that in heightening public awareness they have also lightened burden that they have been quietly bearing for so many years.

To them I pledge to do all that I can to ensure that their daughters and granddaughters never share their experiences. Over the past few weeks, I have been emphatic that the Senate has an obligation to investigate and evaluate the serious allegations of sexual assault. I called for and supported the additional hearing to hear from both Prof. Ford and Judge Kavanaugh. I also pushed for and supported the FBI's supplemental background check investigation. This was the right thing to do.

Christine Ford never sought the spotlight. She indicated that she was terrified to appear before the Senate Judiciary Committee, and she has shunned attention since then. She seemed completely unaware of Chairman Grassley's offer to allow her to testify confidentially in California. Watching her, Mr. President, I could not help but feel that some people who wanted to engineer the defeat of this nomination cared little, if at all, for her well-being.

Prof. Ford testified that a very limited of number people had access to her letter, yet that letter found its way into the public domain. She testified that she never gave permission for that very private letter to be released, and yet here we are. We are in the middle of a fight that she never sought, arguing about claims that she wanted to raise confidentially.

Now, one theory I've heard espoused repeatedly is that our colleague Sen. Feinstein leaked Prof. Ford's letter at the 11th hour to derail this process. I want to state this very clearly. I know Senator Dianne Feinstein extremely well, and I believe that she would never do that. I knew that to be the case before she even stated it at the hearing. She is a person of integrity and I stand by her.

I have also heard some argue that the chairman of the committee somehow treated Prof. Ford unfairly. Nothing could be further from the truth. Chairman Grassley along with his excellent staff treated Prof. Ford with compassion and respect throughout the entire process. And that is the way the senator from Iowa has conducted himself throughout a lifetime dedicated to public service.

But the fact remains, Mr. President, someone leaked this letter against professor Ford's expressed wishes. I suspect regrettably that we will never know for certain who did it. To that leaker who I hope is listening now, let me say that what you did was unconscionable. You have taken a survivor who was not only entitled to your respect but who also trusted you to protect her, and you have sacrificed her well-being in a misguided attempt to win whatever political crusade you think you are fighting.

My only hope is that your callous act has turned this process into such a dysfunctional circus that it will cause the Senate and indeed all Americans to reconsider how we evaluate Supreme Court if that happens, then the appalling lack of compassion you afforded Prof. Ford will at least have some unintended positive consequences.

Mr. President, the politically charged atmosphere surrounding this nomination has reached a fever pitch even before these allegations were known, and it has been challenging even then to separate fact from fiction. We live in a time of such great disunity as the bitter fight over this nomination both in the Senate and among the public clearly demonstrates. It is not merely a case of differing groups having different opinions. It is a case of people bearing extreme ill will toward those who disagree with them. In our intense focus on our differences, we have forgotten the common values that bind us together as Americans.

When some of our best minds are seeking to develop even more sophisticated algorithms designed to link us to websites that only reinforce and cater to our views, we can only expect our differences to intensify. This would have alarmed the drafters of our constitution who were acutely aware that different values and interests could prevent Americans from becoming and remaining a single people.

Indeed, of the six objectives they invoked in the Preamble to the Constitution, the one that they put first was the formation of a more perfect union. Their vision of a more perfect union does not exist today if anything, we appear to be moving farther away from it. It is particularly worrisome that the Supreme Court, the institution that most Americans see as the principle guardian of our shared constitutional heritage is viewed as part of the problem through a political lens.

Mr. President, we've heard a lot of charges and countercharges about Judge Kavanaugh, but as those who have known him best have attested, he has been an exemplary public servant, judge, teacher, coach, husband, and father. Despite the turbulent, bitter fight surrounding his nomination, my fervent hope is that Brett Kavanaugh will work to lessen the divisions in the Supreme Court so that we have far fewer 5 to 4 decisions and so that public confidence in our judiciary and our highest court is restored.

Mr. President, I will vote to confirm Judge Kavanaugh. Thank you, Mr. President."

October 5, 2018
Senator Susan Collins, Maine.
U.S. Senate, Assembled.

Barack Obama served as the 44th President of the United States. His story is the American story—values from the heartland, a middle-class upbringing in a strong family, hard work and education as the means of getting ahead, and the conviction that a life so blessed should be lived in service to others.

The Constitution and Race

If you look at the victories and failures of the civil rights movement and its litigation strategy in the court, I think where it succeeded was to invest formal rights in previously dispossessed people, so that now I would have the right to vote. I would now be able to sit at the lunch counter and order and as long as I could pay for it I'd be OK.

But, the Supreme Court never ventured into the issues of redistribution of wealth, and of more basic issues such as political and economic justice in society. To that extent, as radical as I think people try to characterize the Warren Court, it wasn't that radical. It didn't break free from the essential constraints that were placed by the Founding Fathers in the Constitution, at least as it's been interpreted, and the Warren Court interpreted in the same way, that generally the Constitution is a charter of negative liberties. Says what the states can't do to you. Says what the federal government can't do to you, but doesn't say what the federal government or state government must do on your behalf.

And that hasn't shifted and one of the, I think, tragedies of the civil rights movement was because the civil rights movement became so court-focused I think there was a tendency to lose track of the political and community organizing and activities on the ground that are able to put together the actual coalition of powers through which you bring about redistributive change. In some ways we still suffer from that.

—President Barack Obama, 2001

James Madison Jr. was an American statesman and Founding Father who served as the fourth president of the United States from 1809 to 1817. He is hailed as the "Father of the Constitution" for his pivotal role in drafting and promoting the United States Constitution and the Bill of Rights.

Gilbert Stuart (1755–1828)
Oil on canvas, 1804
The Colonial Williamsburg Foundation

Introduction

by David Osterlund

Throughout the steamy Philadelphia summer of 1787, the fifty-five delegates to the Constitutional Convention often feared that all was lost. Disgusted, some returned home; but others remained to compromise . . . and compromise . . . and compromise. The questions seemed endless. Would big states dominate the small? Who had the power to tax? What are property rights? Then there were issues of trade, treaties, banks, westward expansion and the festering institution of slavery. In the end, the "Framers" agreed on a document whose objectives were set forth in the name of "We the People" to "establish justice, insure domestic Tranquility, provide for the common defence, promote the general Welfare, and secure the Blessings of Liberty to ourselves and our Posterity. . . ." Without bloodshed, this document overturned the Articles of Confederation and created the nation we now hold in trust for future generations. The bedrock of America's success has been this enduring Constitution and the remarkable representative democracy that it has fostered.

It is a practical document, drawn up by practical men facing practical problems. Those Framers applied to their task a thorough familiarity with history, a subtle understanding of human nature, and an evident respect for the English language. But their handiwork has persisted and endured, not because of its theoretical coherence, or the elegant symmetry of the federal structure it created, or of its graceful prose, but because it has worked. Worked for millions of people of different origins, races and religions.

The Constitution succeeded in solving the pressing problems the young nation faced in 1787. With necessary amendments, it has continued to provide a means for a nation, grown ever more powerful, prosperous, and complex, to grapple with the difficulties presented to it by a dangerous and interdependent world.

Its future will depend on the ability of a self-governing nation of free men and women to find within this rich and living charter the way to confront the challenges of the centuries ahead. An active and informed Citizenry is necessary to the effective functioning of our constitutional system. As our first Chief Justice John Marshall wrote, "The people make the Constitution, and the people can unmake it. It is the creature of their own will and lives only by their will." All of us have an obligation to study the Constitution and participate actively in the system of self-government it establishes. This is an obligation we owe not only to ourselves and to our posterity, but to the Framers, who risked everything for freedom, and to the brave men and women who throughout our history have preserved the Constitution, often at the cost of their lives. Let us rededicate ourselves to the values the Constitution embodies.

—June 13, 1995

George Washington was an American political leader, military general, statesman, freemason and Founding Father who served as the first president of the United States. He commanded Patriot forces in the new nation's vital American Revolutionary War and led them to victory over the British.

year. — The difference in the quality of these, though there was no perceivable [difference] in the quality of the soil previous to the preceeding crops, was so apparent as to be discovered almost as far as the field could be seen. — Those on the Potatoe ground being so much the most luxuriant.

It would seem, from the public Gazettes, that the minority in your State are preparing for another attack of the — now — adopted Government; how formidable it may be, I know not. But that Providence which has hitherto smiled on the honest endeavours of the well meaning part of the People of this Country will not, I trust, withdraw its support from them at this crisis. — With best respects to Mrs Peters & yourself, in which Mrs Washington joins me, I am — Dear Sir

Your most Obedt

Humble Servant

Go: Washington

Richard Peters Esqr.

George Washington's Letter on God and the Constitution

September 7th, 1788

George Washington:

> "It Was the Divine 'Providence' of God that Guided the Americans Through the Revolution, Victory, and the Adoption of the Newly Adopted Constitution and He Prays that the Same Providence Will Continue to Sustain Them Now That That Constitution Is Under Attack."

Written a week after he informed Alexander Hamilton that he would likely accept calls to assume the Presidency

> *"That Providence which has hitherto smiled on the honest endeavors of the well meaning part of the People of this Country will not, I trust, withdraw its support from them at this crisis."*

Benjamin Franklin was an American polymath and one of the Founding Fathers of the United States. Franklin was a leading author, printer, political theorist, politician, freemason, postmaster, scientist, inventor, humorist, civic activist, statesman, and diplomat. As a scientist, he was a major figure in the American Enlightenment and the history of physics for his discoveries and theories regarding electricity. As an inventor, he is known for the lightning rod, bifocals, and the Franklin stove, among other inventions. He founded many civic organizations, including the Library Company, Philadelphia's first fire department and the University of Pennsylvania.

Benjamin Franklin's Final Speech in the Constitutional Convention from the notes of James Madison

Mr. President:

I confess that I do not entirely approve of this Constitution at present, but Sir, I am not sure I shall never approve it: For having lived long, I have experienced many Instances of being oblig'd, by better Information or fuller Consideration, to change Opinions even on important Subjects, which I once thought right, but found to be otherwise. It is therefore that the older I grow the more apt I am to doubt my own Judgment, and to pay more Respect to the Judgment of others. Most Men indeed as well as most Sects in Religion, think themselves in Possession of all Truth, and that wherever others differ from them it is so far Error. Steele, a Protestant in a Dedication tells the Pope, that the only Difference between our two Churches in their Opinions of the Certainty of their Doctrine, is, the Romish Church is infallible, and the Church of England is never in the Wrong. But tho' many private Persons think almost as highly of their own Infallibility, as of that of their Sect, few express it so naturally as a certain French Lady, who in a little Dispute with her Sister, said, I don't know how it happens, Sister, but I meet with no body but myself that's always in the right. Il n'y a que moi qui a toujours raison.

In these Sentiments, Sir, I agree to this Constitution, with all its Faults, if they are such; because I think a General Government necessary for us, and there is no Form of Government but what may be a Blessing to the People if well administered; and I believe farther that this is likely to be well administered for a Course of Years, and can only end in Despotism as other Forms have done before it, when the People shall become so corrupted as to need Despotic Government, being incapable of any other.

I doubt too whether any other Convention we can obtain, may be able to make a better Constitution: For when you assemble a Number of Men to have the Advantage of their joint Wisdom, you inevitably assemble with those Men all their Prejudices, their Passions, their Errors of Opinion, their local Interests, and their selfish Views. From such an Assembly can a perfect Production be expected? It therefore astonishes me, Sir, to find this System approaching so near to Perfection as it does; and I think it will astonish our Enemies, who are waiting with Confidence to hear that our Councils are confounded, like those of the Builders of Babel, and that our States are on the Point of Separation, only to meet hereafter for the Purpose of cutting one another's throats. Thus I consent, Sir, to this Constitution because I expect no better, and because I am not sure that it is not the best.

The Opinions I have had of its Errors, I sacrifice to the Public Good. I have never whispered a Syllable of them abroad. Within these Walls they were born, and here they shall die. If every one of us in returning to our Constituents were to report the Objections he has had to it, and use his Influence to gain Partisan in support of them, we might prevent its being generally received, and thereby lose all the salutary Effects and great Advantages resulting naturally in our favour among foreign Nations, as well as among ourselves, from our real or apparent Unanimity. Much of the Strength and Efficiency of any Government, in procuring and securing Happiness to the People depends on Opinion, on the general Opinion of the Goodness of that Government as well as of the Wisdom and Integrity of its Governors. I hope therefore that for our own Sakes, as a Part of the People, and for the sake of our Posterity, we shall act heartily and unanimously in recommending this Constitution, wherever our Influence may extend, and turn our future Thoughts and Endeavours to the Means of having it well administered.

On the whole, Sir, I cannot help expressing a Wish, that every Member of the Convention, who may still have Objections to it, would with me on this Occasion doubt a little of his own Infallibility, and to make manifest our Unanimity, put his Name to this instrument.

Warren Earl Burger was the 15th Chief Justice of the United States, serving from 1969 to 1986. Born in Saint Paul, Minnesota, Burger graduated from the St. Paul College of Law in 1931. He helped secure the Minnesota delegation's support for Dwight D. Eisenhower at the 1952 Republican National Convention.

Why We Revere the Constitution

by The Late Warren E. Burger
Chief Justice of the United States
Supreme Court, 1969-1986

A century ago, Lord Bryce, one of the most quoted European observers of American life, wrote in *The American Constitution*:

> The Constitution . . . deserves the veneration with which Americans have been accustomed to regard it. It is true that many criticisms have been passed on its arrangement, upon its omissions . . . Yet, after all deductions it ranks above every other written constitution for the intrinsic excellence of its scheme, its adaptation to the circumstances of the people, its simplicity, brevity, and precision of its language, its judicious mixture of definiteness in principle with elasticity in details.

This well expresses the genius and the spirit of our Constitution, which has emerged intact through two centuries that have seen our own civil war, two world wars, forty years of "cold war," a worldwide depression, and tremendous technological change. . . . [Ilt is useful to reflect upon some particular features of that document that now seem commonplace but when they were first proposed seemed to many people revolutionary, idealistic, and unworkable.

There are at least four such features. First, the Constitution represented not a grant of power from rulers to the people ruled—as with King John's grant of the Magna Charta at Runnymede in 1215—but a grant of power by the people to a government which they had created. No other national government before that time was based upon such a concept. Until then, monarchs ruled by divine right and their subjects had only those privileges which their rulers saw fit to bestow upon them. The work of those fifty-five men at Philadelphia during the summer of 1787 marked the beginning of the end of the divine right of kings as well as many of the rigid class distinctions that went along with it.

Second, the government created by the Constitution had a system of checks and balances that had never been tried in a national government. Drawing on the ideas of Locke, Montesquieu, and the Scottish Enlightenment, the Framers of the Constitution recognized that even officers elected by the people or appointed by the people's representatives might abuse their powers. Like the farmers of their day, they knew that the value of a horse or an ox depended on the harness. Accordingly, the Constitution provided for both a horizontal and a vertical separation of powers: The national government was divided into three coequal, coordinate branches, and the state governments were to provide a counterweight to the national government. Our own experience demonstrates that such a structure does not necessarily produce the most efficient government, but freedom, not efficiency, was the primary objective. After all, the hope of freedom and opportunity was what brought the early Americans from Europe to this continent. The American system of separated powers and checks and balances has proved to be one of the most important and effective means of ensuring the individual liberty the Framers sought.

Third, the drafters of the Constitution were able to strike a proper balance between a strong government and one that leaves them free to do as they please. Thomas Jefferson had frequently pointed out the tension between these two values. As colonists, the delegates had experienced the tyranny of a strong but distant and unresponsive government. During and after the revolution, they had experienced the opposite extreme: The federal government under the Articles of Confederation did not interfere with individual liberty, but it was barely adequate to carry on the war. It had no power to levy or enforce taxes and no authority to raise armies, a situation that brought the colonists perilously close to losing the revolution. The structure of ordered liberty created by the Constitution combined the strength of the British system with great individual freedom.

Fourth, the new Constitution. largely through its Commerce Clause, gave us a "common market" a century and a half before that phrase came into our vocabulary with the advent of the European economic community. During the years following the American Revolution and immediately prior to the drafting of the Constitution, there were serious limits on commerce between the thirteen sovereign states. Each state was free to set up trade barriers and to issue its own currency. Some states treated citizens of other states as aliens. The Constitution created a strong central authority that ensured free trade among the states and with other nations and provided a common currency, a central revenue system, and a central banking system, all of which were essential if the previously sovereign, independent states were to develop into a true nation and a powerful economic force.

These and other features of the Constitution account for its durability and vitality over the past two hundred years. During that short period, this nation has grown from a small contingent of less than four million people, scattered along the eastern seaboard, into a country of nearly 230 million and a great world power. Other nations had industrious, talented, and ambitious citizens, but the unique system created by the Constitution allowed every person to develop his or her God-given talents and abilities without being burdened by the heavy hand of arbitrary government or ancient traditions. It thereby unleashed the full energies of the American people. The Constitution—combined with the strength of our people, with personal integrity, with individual responsibility, and with the traditions of home and family—has permitted us to enjoy unprecedented freedom and prosperity, and has served as a model for countless other governments formed by freedom-loving people around the world.

James Madison, looking back on the creation of the Constitution, observed, "It is impossible for the man of pious reflection not to perceive . . . a finger of that Almighty Hand, which has been so frequently and signally extended to our relief in the critical stages of the revolution." The Constitution was indeed a watershed in the history of governments and, more important, in humanity's struggle for freedom and fulfillment. It behooves all of us to read it, understand it, revere it, and vigorously defend it.

George Washington as Statesman at the Constitutional Convention. Oil on canvas by Junius Brutus Steams. Courtesy of the Virginia Museum of Fine Arts, 1856. On September 17, 1787, 38 delegates signed the Constitution.

— The —
Constitution of the United States of America

NOTE:
The punctuation and spelling of the text of the Constitution and Amendments as they appear in this book are consistent with those of the original documents.

— The —
Constitution of the United States of America

We the People of the United States, in Order to form a more perfect Union, establish Justice, insure domestic Tranquility, provide for the common defence, promote the general Welfare, and secure the Blessings of Liberty to ourselves and our Posterity, do ordain and establish this Constitution for the United States of America.

ARTICLE I
(Article 1 - Legislative)

Section 1

All legislative Powers herein granted shall be vested in a Congress of the United States, which shall consist of a Senate and House of Representatives.

Section 2

The House of Representatives shall be composed of Members chosen every second Year by the People of the several States, and the Electors in each State shall have the Qualifications requisite for Electors of the most numerous Branch of the State Legislature.

No Person shall be a Representative who shall not have attained to the Age of twenty five Years, and been seven Years a Citizen of the United States, and who shall not, when elected, be an Inhabitant of that State in which he shall be chosen.

[Representatives and direct Taxes shall be apportioned among the several States which may be included within this Union, according to their respective Numbers, which shall be determined by adding to the whole Number of free Persons, including those bound to Service for a Term of Years, and excluding Indians not taxed, three fifths of all other Persons.]* The actual Enumeration shall be made within three Years after the first Meeting of the Congress of the United States, and within every subsequent Term of ten Years, in such Manner as they shall by Law direct. The Number of Representatives shall not exceed one for every thirty Thousand, but each State shall have at Least one Representative; and until such enumeration shall be made, the State of New Hampshire shall be entitled to chuse three, Massachusetts eight, Rhode-Island and Providence Plantations one, Connecticut five, New-York six, New Jersey four, Pennsylvania eight, Delaware one, Maryland six, Virginia ten, North Carolina five, South Carolina five, and Georgia three.

When vacancies happen in the Representation from any State, the Executive Authority thereof shall issue Writs of Election to fill such Vacancies.

The House of Representatives shall chuse their Speaker and other Officers; and shall have the sole Power of Impeachment.

Section 3

The Senate of the United States shall be composed of two Senators from each State, [chosen by the

* Changed by section 2 of the Fourteenth Amendment.

Legislature thereof,]* for six Years; and each Senator shall have one Vote.

Immediately after they shall be assembled in Consequence of the first Election, they shall be divided as equally as may be into three Classes. The Seats of the Senators of the first Class shall be vacated at the Expiration of the second Year, of the second Class at the Expiration of the fourth Year, and of the third Class at the Expiration of the sixth Year, so that one third may be chosen every second Year; and if Vacancies happen by Resignation, or otherwise, during the Recess of the Legislature of any State, the Executive thereof may make temporary Appointments until the next Meeting of the Legislature, which shall then fill such Vacancies.**

No Person shall be a Senator who shall not have attained to the Age of thirty Years, and been nine Years a Citizen of the United States, and who shall not, when elected, be an Inhabitant of that State for which he shall be chosen.

The Vice President of the United States shall be President of the Senate, but shall have no Vote, unless they be equally divided.

The Senate shall chuse their other Officers, and also a President pro tempore, in the Absence of the Vice President, or when he shall exercise the Office of President of the United States.

The Senate shall have the sole Power to try all Impeachments. When sitting for that Purpose, they shall be

* Changed by section 1 of the Seventeenth Amendment.

** Changed by section 2 of the Seventeenth Amendment.

on Oath or Affirmation. When the President of the United States is tried, the Chief Justice shall preside: And no Person shall be convicted without the Concurrence of two thirds of the Members present.

Judgment in Cases of impeachment shall not extend further than to removal from Office, and disqualification to hold and enjoy any Office of honor, Trust or Profit under the United States: but the Party convicted shall nevertheless be liable and subject to Indictment, Trial, Judgment and Punishment, according to Law.

Section 4

The Times, Places and Manner of holding Elections for Senators and Representatives, shall be prescribed in each State by the Legislature thereof; but the Congress may at any time by Law make or alter such Regulations, except as to the Places of chusing Senators.

The Congress shall assemble at least once in every Year, and such Meeting shall be [on the first Monday in December,]* unless they shall by Law appoint a different Day.

Section 5

Each House shall be the Judge of the Elections, Returns and Qualifications of its own Members, and a Majority of each shall constitute a Quorum to do Business; but a smaller Number may adjourn from day to day, and may be

* Changed by section 2 of the Twentieth Amendment.

authorized to compel the Attendance of absent Members, in such Manner, and under such Penalties as each House may provide.

Each House may determine the Rules of its Proceedings, punish its Members for disorderly Behaviour, and, with the Concurrence of two thirds, expel a Member.

Each House shall keep a Journal of its Proceedings, and from time to time publish the same, excepting such Parts as may in their Judgment require Secrecy; and the Yeas and Nays of the Members of either House on any question shall, at the Desire of one fifth of those Present, be entered on the Journal.

Neither House, during the Session of Congress, shall, without the Consent of the other, adjourn for more than three days, nor to any other Place than that in which the two Houses shall be sitting.

Section 6

The Senators and Representatives shall receive a Compensation for their Services, to be ascertained by Law, and paid out of the Treasury of the United States.6 They shall in all Cases, except Treason, Felony and Breach of the Peace, be privileged from Arrest during their Attendance at the Session of their respective Houses, and in going to and returning from the same; and for any Speech or Debate in either House, they shall not be questioned in any other Place.

No Senator or Representative shall, during the Time for

which he was elected, be appointed to any civil Office under the Authority of the United States, which shall have been created, or the Emoluments whereof shall have been encreased during such time; and no Person holding any Office under the United States, shall be a Member of either House during his Continuance in Office.

Section 7

All Bills for raising Revenue shall originate in the House of Representatives; but the Senate may propose or concur with Amendments as on other Bills.

Every Bill which shall have passed the House of Representatives and the Senate, shall, before it become a Law, be presented to the President of the United States; If he approve he shall sign it, but if not he shall return it, with his Objections to that House in which it shall have originated, who shall enter the Objections at large on their Journal, and proceed to reconsider it. If after such Reconsideration two thirds of that House shall agree to pass the Bill, it shall be sent, together with the Objections, to the other House, by which it shall likewise be reconsidered, and if approved by two thirds of that House, it shall become a Law. But in all such Cases the Votes of both Houses shall be determined by yeas and Nays, and the Names of the Persons voting for and against the Bill shall be entered on the Journal of each House respectively. If any Bill shall not be returned by the President within ten Days (Sundays excepted) after it shall have been presented to him, the Same shall be a Law, in like Manner as if he had signed it, unless the Congress by their Adjournment prevent its

Return, in which Case it shall not be a Law.

Every Order, Resolution, or Vote to which the Concurrence of the Senate and House of Representatives may be necessary (except on a question of Adjournment) shall be presented to the President of the United States; and before the Same shall take Effect, shall be approved by him, or being disapproved by him, shall be repassed by two thirds of the Senate and House of Representatives, according to the Rules and Limitations prescribed in the Case of a Bill.

Section 8

The Congress shall have Power To lay and collect Taxes, Duties, Imposts and Excises, to pay the Debts and provide for the common Defence and general Welfare of the United States; but all Duties, Imposts and Excises shall be uniform throughout the United States;

To borrow Money on the credit of the United States;

To regulate Commerce with foreign Nations, and among the several States, and with the Indian Tribes;

To establish an uniform Rule of Naturalization, and uniform Laws on the subject of Bankruptcies throughout the United States;

To coin Money, regulate the Value thereof, and of foreign Coin, and fix the Standard of Weights and Measures;

To provide for the Punishment of counterfeiting the Securities and current Coin of the United States;

To establish Post Offices and post Roads;

To promote the Progress of Science and useful Arts, by securing for limited Times to Authors and Inventors the exclusive Right to their respective Writings and Discoveries;

To constitute Tribunals inferior to the supreme Court;

To define and punish Piracies and Felonies committed on the high Seas, and Offences against the Law of Nations;

To declare War, grant Letters of Marque and Reprisal, and make Rules concerning Captures on Land and Water;

To raise and support Armies, but no Appropriation of Money to that Use shall be for a longer Term than two Years;

To provide and maintain a Navy;

To make Rules for the Government and Regulation of the land and naval Forces;

To provide for calling forth the Militia to execute the Laws of the Union, suppress Insurrections and repel Invasions;

To provide for organizing, arming, and disciplining, the Militia, and for governing such Part of them as may be employed in the Service of the United States, reserving to the States respectively, the Appointment of the Officers, and the Authority of training the Militia according to the discipline prescribed by Congress;

To exercise exclusive Legislation in all Cases whatsoever, over such District (not exceeding ten Miles square) as may, by Cession of particular States, and the Acceptance of Congress, become the Seat of the Government of the United States, and to exercise like Authority over all Places purchased by the Consent of the Legislature of the State in which the Same shall be, for the Erection of Forts, Magazines, Arsenals, dock-Yards, and other needful Buildings;—And

To make all Laws which shall be necessary and proper for carrying into Execution the foregoing Powers, and all other Powers vested by this Constitution in the

Government of the United States, or in any Department or Officer thereof.

Section 9

The Migration or Importation of such Persons as any of the States now existing shall think proper to admit, shall not be prohibited by the Congress prior to the Year one thousand eight hundred and eight, but a Tax or duty may be imposed on such Importation, not exceeding ten dollars for each Person.

The Privilege of the Writ of Habeas Corpus shall not be suspended, unless when in Cases of Rebellion or Invasion the public Safety may require it.

No Bill of Attainder or *ex post facto* Law shall be passed.

No Capitation, or other direct, Tax shall be laid, unless in Proportion to the Census or Enumeration herein before directed to be taken.7

No Tax or Duty shall be laid on Articles exported from any State.

No Preference shall be given by any Regulation of Commerce or Revenue to the Ports of one State over those of another: nor shall Vessels bound to, or from, one State, be obliged to enter, clear, or pay Duties in another.

No Money shall be drawn from the Treasury, but in Consequence of Appropriations made by Law; and a regular Statement and Account of the Receipts and Expenditures of all public Money shall be published from time to time.

No Title of Nobility shall be granted by the United States: And no Person holding any Office of Profit or Trust under them, shall, without the Consent of the Congress, accept of any present, Emolument, Office, or Title, of any kind whatever, from any King, Prince, or foreign State.

Section 10

No State shall enter into any Treaty, Alliance, or Confederation; grant Letters of Marque and Reprisal; coin Money; emit Bills of Credit; make any Thing but gold and silver Coin a Tender in Payment of Debts; pass any Bill of Attainder, *ex post facto* Law, or Law impairing the Obligation of Contracts, or grant any Title of Nobility.

No State shall, without the Consent of the Congress, lay any Imposts or Duties on Imports or Exports, except what may be absolutely necessary for executing it's inspection Laws: and the net Produce of all Duties and Imposts, laid by any State on Imports or Exports, shall be for the Use of the Treasury of the United States; and all such Laws shall be subject to the Revision and Controul of the Congress.

No State shall, without the Consent of Congress, lay any Duty of Tonnage, keep Troops, or Ships of War in time of Peace, enter into any Agreement or Compact with another State, or with a foreign Power, or engage in War, unless actually invaded, or in such imminent Danger as will not admit of delay.

ARTICLE II
(Article 2 - Executive)

Section 1

The executive Power shall be vested in a President of the United States of America. He shall hold his Office during the Term of four Years, and, together with the Vice President, chosen for the same Term, be elected, as follows

Each State shall appoint, in such Manner as the Legislature thereof may direct, a Number of Electors, equal to the whole Number of Senators and Representatives to which the State may be entitled in the Congress: but no Senator or Representative, or Person holding an Office of Trust or Profit under the United States, shall be appointed an Elector.

[The Electors shall meet in their respective States, and vote by Ballot for two Persons, of whom one at least shall not be an Inhabitant of the same State with themselves. And they shall make a List of all the Persons voted for, and of the Number of Votes for each; which List they shall sign and certify, and transmit sealed to the Seat of the Government of the United States, directed to the President of the Senate. The President of the Senate shall, in the Presence of the Senate and House of Representatives, open all the Certificates, and the Votes shall then be counted. The Person having the greatest Number of Votes shall be the President, if such Number be a Majority of the whole

Number of Electors appointed; and if there be more than one who have such Majority, and have an equal Number of Votes, then the House of Representatives shall immediately chuse by Ballot one of them for President; and if no Person have a Majority, then from the five highest on the List the said House shall in like Manner chuse the President. But in chusing the President, the Votes shall be taken by States, the Representation from each State having one Vote; A quorum for this Purpose shall consist of a Member or Members from two thirds of the States, and a Majority of all the States shall be necessary to a Choice. In every Case, after the Choice of the President, the Person having the greatest Number of Votes of the Electors shall be the Vice President. But if there should remain two or more who have equal Votes, the Senate shall chuse from them by Ballot the Vice President.]*

The Congress may determine the Time of chusing the Electors, and the Day on which they shall give their Votes; which Day shall be the same throughout the United States.

No Person except a natural born Citizen, or a Citizen of the United States, at the time of the Adoption of this Constitution, shall be eligible to the Office of President; neither shall any Person be eligible to that Office who shall not have attained to the Age of thirty five Years, and been fourteen Years a Resident within the United States.

[In Case of the Removal of the President from Office, or of his Death, Resignation, or Inability to discharge the Powers and Duties of the said Office, the Same shall devolve on the Vice President, and the Congress may by Law provide for the Case of Removal, Death, Resignation or Inability,

* Superseded by the Twelfth Amendment.

both of the President and Vice President, declaring what Officer shall then act as President, and such Officer shall act accordingly, until the Disability be removed, or a President shall be elected.]*

The President shall, at stated Times, receive for his Services, a Compensation, which shall neither be encreased nor diminished during the Period for which he shall have been elected, and he shall not receive within that Period any other Emolument from the United States, or any of them.

Before he enter on the Execution of his Office, he shall take the following Oath or Affirmation:—"I do solemnly swear (or affirm) that I will faithfully execute the Office of President of the United States, and will to the best of my Ability, preserve, protect and defend the Constitution of the United States."

Section 2

The President shall be Commander in Chief of the Army and Navy of the United States, and of the Militia of the several States, when called into the actual Service of the United States; he may require the Opinion, in writing, of the principal Officer in each of the executive Departments, upon any Subject relating to the Duties of their respective Offices, and he shall have Power to grant Reprieves and Pardons for Offences against the United States, except in Cases of Impeachment.

He shall have Power, by and with the Advice and Consent of the Senate, to make Treaties, provided two

* Modified by the Twenty-Fifth Amendment.

thirds of the Senators present concur; and he shall nominate, and by and with the Advice and Consent of the Senate, shall appoint Ambassadors, other public Ministers and Consuls, Judges of the supreme Court, and all other Officers of the United States, whose Appointments are not herein otherwise provided for, and which shall be established by Law: but the Congress may by Law vest the Appointment of such inferior Officers, as they think proper, in the President alone, in the Courts of Law, or in the Heads of Departments.

The President shall have Power to fill up all Vacancies that may happen during the Recess of the Senate, by granting Commissions which shall expire at the End of their next Session.

Section 3

He shall from time to time give to the Congress Information of the State of the Union, and recommend to their Consideration such Measures as he shall judge necessary and expedient; he may, on extraordinary Occasions, convene both Houses, or either of them, and in Case of Disagreement between them, with Respect to the Time of Adjournment, he may adjourn them to such Time as he shall think proper; he shall receive Ambassadors and other public Ministers; he shall take Care that the Laws be faithfully executed, and shall Commission all the Officers of the United States.

Section 4

The President, Vice President and all civil Officers of the United States, shall be removed from Office on Impeachment for, and Conviction of, Treason, Bribery, or other high Crimes and Misdemeanors.

ARTICLE III
(Article 3 - Judicial)

Section 1

The judicial Power of the United States, shall be vested in one supreme Court, and in such inferior Courts as the Congress may from time to time ordain and establish. The Judges, both of the supreme and inferior Courts, shall hold their Offices during good Behaviour, and shall, at stated Times, receive for their Services, a Compensation, which shall not be diminished during their Continuance in Office.

Section 2

The judicial Power shall extend to all Cases, in Law and Equity, arising under this Constitution, the Laws of the United States, and Treaties made, or which shall be made, under their Authority;—to all Cases affecting Ambassadors, other public Ministers and Consuls;—to all Cases of admiralty and maritime Jurisdiction;—to Controversies to which the United States shall be a Party;—to Controversies between two or more States;—between a State and Citizens of another State;10 —between Citizens of different States, —between Citizens of the same State claiming Lands under Grants of different States, and between a State, or the Citizens thereof, and foreign States, Citizens or Subjects.

In all Cases affecting Ambassadors, other public Ministers and Consuls, and those in which a State shall be Party, the supreme Court shall have original Jurisdiction. In all the other Cases before mentioned, the supreme Court shall have appellate Jurisdiction, both as to Law and Fact, with such Exceptions, and under such Regulations as the Congress shall make.

The Trial of all Crimes, except in Cases of Impeachment, shall be by Jury; and such Trial shall be held in the State where the said Crimes shall have been committed; but when not committed within any State, the Trial shall be at such Place or Places as the Congress may by Law have directed.

Section 3

Treason against the United States, shall consist only in levying War against them, or in adhering to their Enemies, giving them Aid and Comfort. No Person shall be convicted of Treason unless on the Testimony of two Witnesses to the same overt Act, or on Confession in open Court.

The Congress shall have Power to declare the Punishment of Treason, but no Attainder of Treason shall work Corruption of Blood, or Forfeiture except during the Life of the Person attainted.

Article IV
(Article 4 - States' Relations)

Section 1

Full Faith and Credit shall be given in each State to the public Acts, Records, and judicial Proceedings of every other State. And the Congress may by general Laws prescribe the Manner in which such Acts, Records and Proceedings shall be proved, and the Effect thereof.

Section 2

The Citizens of each State shall be entitled to all Privileges and Immunities of Citizens in the several States.

A Person charged in any State with Treason, Felony, or other Crime, who shall flee from Justice, and be found in another State, shall on Demand of the executive Authority of the State from which he fled, be delivered up, to be removed to the State having Jurisdiction of the Crime.

[No Person held to Service or Labour in one State, under the Laws thereof, escaping into another, shall, in Consequence of any Law or Regulation therein, be discharged from such Service or Labour, but shall be delivered up on Claim of the Party to whom such Service or Labour may be due.]*

* Superseded by the Thirteenth Amendment.

Section 3

New States may be admitted by the Congress into this Union; but no new State shall be formed or erected within the Jurisdiction of any other State; nor any State be formed by the Junction of two or more States, or Parts of States, without the Consent of the Legislatures of the States concerned as well as of the Congress.

The Congress shall have Power to dispose of and make all needful Rules and Regulations respecting the Territory or other Property belonging to the United States; and nothing in this Constitution shall be so construed as to Prejudice any Claims of the United States, or of any particular State.

Section 4

The United States shall guarantee to every State in this Union a Republican Form of Government, and shall protect each of them against Invasion; and on Application of the Legislature, or of the Executive (when the Legislature cannot be convened) against domestic Violence.

Article V
(Article 5 - Mode of Amendment)

The Congress, whenever two thirds of both Houses shall deem it necessary, shall propose Amendments to this Constitution, or, on the Application of the Legislatures of two thirds of the several States, shall call a Convention for proposing Amendments, which, in either Case, shall be valid to all Intents and Purposes, as Part of this Constitution, when ratified by the Legislatures of three fourths of the several States, or by Conventions in three fourths thereof, as the one or the other Mode of Ratification may be proposed by the Congress; Provided that no Amendment which may be made prior to the Year One thousand eight hundred and eight shall in any Manner affect the first and fourth Clauses in the Ninth Section of the first Article; and that no State, without its Consent, shall be deprived of its equal Suffrage in the Senate.

Article VI
(Article 6 - Prior Debts, National Supremacy, Oaths of Office)

All Debts contracted and Engagements entered into, before the Adoption of this Constitution, shall be as valid against the United States under this Constitution, as under the Confederation.

This Constitution, and the Laws of the United States which shall be made in Pursuance thereof; and all Treaties made, or which shall be made, under the Authority of the United States, shall be the supreme Law of the Land; and the Judges in every State shall be bound thereby, any Thing in the Constitution or Laws of any State to the Contrary notwithstanding.

The Senators and Representatives before mentioned, and the Members of the several State Legislatures, and all executive and judicial Officers, both of the United States and of the several States, shall be bound by Oath or Affirmation, to support this Constitution; but no religious Test shall ever be required as a Qualification to any Office or public Trust under the United States.

Article VII
(Article 7 - Ratification)

The Ratification of the Conventions of nine States, shall be sufficient for the Establishment of this Constitution between the States so ratifying the Same.

done in Convention by the Unanimous Consent of the States present the Seventeenth Day of September in the Year of our Lord one thousand seven hundred and Eighty seven and of the Independence of the United States of America the Twelfth In witness whereof We have hereunto subscribed our Names,

Attest William Jackson Secretary

Go: Washington -Presidt. and deputy from Virginia Showing George Washington's signature.

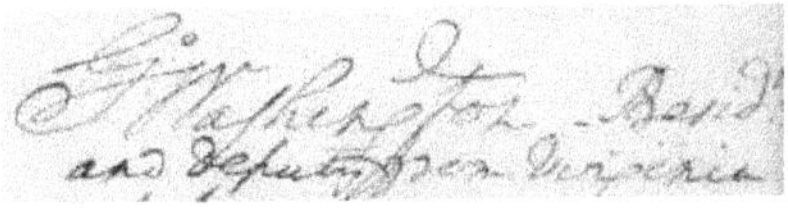

Delaware
Geo: Read
Gunning Bedford jun
John Dickinson
Richard Bassett
Jaco: Broom

Maryland
James McHenry
Dan of St Thos. Jenifer
Danl Carroll.

Virginia
John Blair—
James Madison Jr.

North Carolina
Wm Blount
Richd. Dobbs Spaight.
Hu Williamson

South Carolina
J. Rutledge
Charles Cotesworth Pinckney
Charles Pinckney
Pierce Butler.

Georgia
William Few
Abr Baldwin

New Hampshire
John Langdon
Nicholas Gilman

Massachusetts
Nathaniel Gorham
Rufus King

Connecticut
Wm. Saml. Johnson
Roger Sherman

New York
Alexander Hamilton

New Jersey
Wil. Livingston
David Brearley.
Wm. Paterson.
Jona: Dayton

Pennsylvania
B Franklin
Thomas Mifflin
Robt Morris
Geo. Clymer
Thos. FitzSimons
Jared Ingersoll
James Wilson.
Gouv Morris

Letter of Transmittal
In Convention. Monday September 17th 1787.

Present
The States of
New Hampshire, Massachusetts, Connecticut, Mr. Hamilton from New York, New Jersey, Pennsylvania, Delaware, Maryland, Virginia, North Carolina, South Carolina and Georgia.

Resolved,

That the preceeding Constitution be laid before the United States in Congress assembled, and that it is the Opinion of this Convention, that it should afterwards be submitted to a Convention of Delegates, chosen in each State by the People thereof, under the Recommendation of its Legislature, for their Assent and Ratification; and that each Convention assenting to, and ratifying the Same, should give Notice thereof to the United States in Congress assembled. Resolved, That it is the Opinion of this Convention, that as soon as the Conventions of nine States shall have ratified this Constitution, the United States in Congress assembled should fix a Day on which Electors should be appointed by the States which shall have ratified the same, and a Day on which the Electors should assemble to vote for the President, and the Time and Place for commencing Proceedings under this Constitution.

That after such Publication the Electors should be

appointed, and the Senators and Representatives elected:

That the Electors should meet on the Day fixed for the Election of the President, and should transmit their Votes certified, signed, sealed and directed, as the Constitution requires, to the Secretary of the United States in Congress assembled, that the Senators and Representatives should convene at the Time and Place assigned; that the Senators should appoint a President of the Senate, for the sole Purpose of receiving, opening and counting the Votes for President; and, that after he shall be chosen, the Congress, together with the President, should, without Delay, proceed to execute this Constitution.

By the unanimous Order of the Convention

W. Jackson Secretary.

Go: Washington -Presidt.

Letter of Transmittal to the President of Congress Monday September 17th 1787.

SIR:

We have now the honor to submit to the consideration of the United States in Congress assembled, that Constitution which has appeared to us the most advisable.

The friends of our country have long seen and desired that the power of making war, peace, and treaties, that of levying money, and regulating commerce, and the correspondent executive and judicial authorities, should be fully and effectually vested in the General Government of the Union; but the impropriety of delegating such extensive trust to one body of men is evident: hence results the necessity of a different organization.

It is obviously impracticable in the Federal Government of these States to secure all rights of independent sovereignty to each, and yet provide for the interest and safety of all. Individuals entering into society must give up a share of liberty to preserve the rest. The magnitude of the sacrifice must depend as well on situation and circumstance, as on the object to be obtained. It is at all times difficult to draw with precision the line between those rights which must be surrendered, and those which may be preserved; and, on the present occasion, this difficulty was increased by a difference among the several States as to their situation, extent, habits, and particular interests.

In all our deliberations on this subject, we kept steadily in our view that which appears to us the greatest interest of every true American, the consolidation of our Union, in which is involved our prosperity, felicity, safety—perhaps our national existence. This important consideration, seriously and deeply impressed on our minds, led each State in the Convention to be less rigid on points of inferior magnitude than might have been otherwise expected; and thus, the Constitution which we now present is the result of a spirit of amity, and of that mutual deference and concession, which the peculiarity of our political situation rendered indispensable.

That it will meet the full and entire approbation of every State is not, perhaps, to be expected; but each will, doubtless, consider, that had her interest alone been consulted, the consequences might have been particularly disagreeable or injurious to others; that it is liable to as few exceptions as could reasonably have been expected, we hope and believe; that it may promote the lasting welfare of that Country so dear to us all, and secure her freedom and happiness, is our most ardent wish.

With great respect,
we have the honor to be,
SIR,
your excellency's most obedient and humble servants:
GEORGE WASHINGTON, President.
By the unanimous order of the convention.

His Excellency

the President of Congress.

Amendments to
— The —
Constitution of the United States of America

ARTICLES IN ADDITION TO, AND AMENDMENT OF, THE CONSTITUTION OF THE UNITED STATES OF AMERICA, PROPOSED BY CONGRESS, AND RATIFIED BY THE SEVERAL STATES, PURSUANT TO THE FIFTH ARTICLE OF THE ORIGINAL CONSTITUTION.

ARTICLE [I] *
(Amendment 1 - Freedom of expression and religion) 13

Congress shall make no law respecting an establishment of religion, or prohibiting the free exercise thereof; or abridging the freedom of speech, or of the press; or the right of the people peaceably to assemble, and to petition the Government for a redress of grievances.

* The first ten Amendments (Bill of Rights) were ratified effective December 15, 1791.

ARTICLE [II]
(Amendment 2 - Bearing Arms)

A well regulated Militia, being necessary to the security of a free State, the right of the people to keep and bear Arms, shall not be infringed.

ARTICLE [III]
(Amendment 3 - Quartering Soldiers)

No Soldier shall, in time of peace be quartered in any house, without the consent of the Owner, nor in time of war, but in a manner to be prescribed by law.

ARTICLE [IV]
(Amendment 4 - Search and Seizure)

The right of the people to be secure in their persons, houses, papers, and effects, against unreasonable searches and seizures, shall not be violated, and no Warrants shall issue, but upon probable cause, supported by Oath or affirmation, and particularly describing the place to be searched, and the persons or things to be seized.

ARTICLE [V]
(Amendment 5 - Rights of Persons)

No person shall be held to answer for a capital, or otherwise infamous crime, unless on a presentment or indictment of a Grand Jury, except in cases arising in the land or naval forces, or in the Militia, when in actual service in time of War or public danger; nor shall any person be subject for the same offence to be twice put in jeopardy of life or limb; nor shall be compelled in any criminal case to be a witness against himself, nor be deprived of life, liberty, or property, without due process of law; nor shall private property be taken for public use, without just compensation.

ARTICLE [VI]
(Amendment 6 - Rights of Accused in Criminal Prosecutions)

In all criminal prosecutions, the accused shall enjoy the right to a speedy and public trial, by an impartial jury of the State and district wherein the crime shall have been committed, which district shall have been previously ascertained by law, and to be informed of the nature and cause of the accusation; to be confronted with the witnesses against him; to have compulsory process for obtaining witnesses in his favor, and to have the Assistance of Counsel for his defence.

ARTICLE [VII]
(Amendment 7 - Civil Trials)

In Suits at common law, where the value in controversy shall exceed twenty dollars, the right of trial by jury shall be preserved, and no fact tried by a jury, shall be otherwise re-examined in any Court of the United States, than according to the rules of the common law.

ARTICLE [VIII]
(Amendment 8 - Further Guarantees in Criminal Cases)

Excessive bail shall not be required, nor excessive fines imposed, nor cruel and unusual punishments inflicted.

ARTICLE [IX]
(Amendment 9 - Unenumerated Rights)

The enumeration in the Constitution, of certain rights, shall not be construed to deny or disparage others retained by the people.

ARTICLE [X]
(Amendment 10 - Reserved Powers)

The powers not delegated to the United States by the Constitution, nor prohibited by it to the States, are reserved to the States respectively, or to the people.

Attest,
John Beckley, Clerk of the House of Representatives.
Sam. A. Otis Secretary of the Senate.

Frederick Augustus Muhlenberg Speaker of the House of Representatives.
John Adams, Vice-President of the United States, and President of the Senate.

(end of the Bill of Rights)

[Article XI] *
(Amendment 11 - Suits Against States)

The Judicial power of the United States shall not be construed to extend to any suit in law or equity, commenced or prosecuted against one of the United States by Citizens of another State, or by Citizens or Subjects of any Foreign State.

* The Eleventh Amendment was ratified February 7, 1795.

[Article XII] *
(Amendment 12 - Election of President)

The Electors shall meet in their respective states, and vote by ballot for President and Vice-President, one of whom, at least, shall not be an inhabitant of the same state with themselves; they shall name in their ballots the person voted for as President, and in distinct ballots the person voted for as Vice-President, and they shall make distinct lists of all persons voted for as President, and of all persons voted for as Vice-President, and of the number of votes for each, which lists they shall sign and certify, and transmit sealed to the seat of the government of the United States, directed to the President of the Senate;—The President of the Senate shall, in the presence of the Senate and House of Representatives, open all the certificates and the votes shall then be counted;—The person having the greatest number of votes for President, shall be the President, if such number be a majority of the whole number of Electors appointed; and if no person have such majority, then from the persons having the highest numbers not exceeding three on the list of those voted for as President, the House of Representatives shall choose immediately, by ballot, the President. But in choosing the President, the votes shall be taken by states, the representation from each state having one vote; a quorum for this purpose shall consist of a member or

* The Twelfth Amendment was ratified June 15, 1804.

members from two-thirds of the states, and a majority of all the states shall be necessary to a choice. [And if the House of Representatives shall not choose a President whenever the right of choice shall devolve upon them, before the fourth day of March next following, then the Vice-President shall act as President, as in the case of the death or other constitutional disability of the President.]*

The person having the greatest number of votes as Vice-President, shall be the Vice-President, if such number be a majority of the whole number of Electors appointed, and if no person have a majority, then from the two highest numbers on the list, the Senate shall choose the Vice-President; a quorum for the purpose shall consist of two-thirds of the whole number of Senators, and a majority of the whole number shall be necessary to a choice. But no person constitutionally ineligible to the office of President shall be eligible to that of Vice-President of the United States.

* Superseded by Section 3 of the Twentieth Amendment.

Article XIII *
(Amendment 13 - Slavery and Involuntary Servitude)

Section 1

Neither slavery nor involuntary servitude, except as a punishment for crime whereof the party shall have been duly convicted, shall exist within the United States, or any place subject to their jurisdiction.

Section 2

Congress shall have power to enforce this article by appropriate legislation.

* The Thirteenth Amendment was ratified December 6, 1865.

Article XIV *
(Amendment 14 - Rights Guaranteed: Privileges and Immunities of Citizenship, Due Process, and Equal Protection)

Section 1

All persons born or naturalized in the United States, and subject to the jurisdiction thereof, are citizens of the United States and of the State wherein they reside. No State shall make or enforce any law which shall abridge the privileges or immunities of citizens of the United States; nor shall any State deprive any person of life, liberty, or property, without due process of law; nor deny to any person within its jurisdiction the equal protection of the laws.

Section 2

Representatives shall be apportioned among the several States according to their respective numbers, counting the whole number of persons in each State, excluding Indians not taxed. But when the right to vote at any election for the choice of electors for President and Vice President of the United States, Representatives in Congress, the Executive and Judicial officers of a State, or the members of the Legislature thereof, is denied to any of the male inhabitants

* The Fourteenth Amendment was ratified July 9, 1868.

of such State, being twenty-one years of age,[15] and citizens of the United States, or in any way abridged, except for participation in rebellion, or other crime, the basis of representation therein shall be reduced in the proportion which the number of such male citizens shall bear to the whole number of male citizens twenty-one years of age in such State.

Section 3

No person shall be a Senator or Representative in Congress, or elector of President and Vice President, or hold any office, civil or military, under the United States, or under any State, who, having previously taken an oath, as a member of Congress, or as an officer of the United States, or as a member of any State legislature, or as an executive or judicial officer of any State, to support the Constitution of the United States, shall have engaged in insurrection or rebellion against the same, or given aid or comfort to the enemies thereof. But Congress may by a vote of two-thirds of each House, remove such disability.

Section 4

The validity of the public debt of the United States, authorized by law, including debts incurred for payment of pensions and bounties for services in suppressing insurrection or rebellion, shall not be questioned. But neither the United States nor any State shall assume or pay any debt or obligation incurred in aid of insurrection or rebellion against the United States, or any claim for the loss or emancipation of any slave; but all such debts, obligations and claims shall be held illegal and void.

Section 5

The Congress shall have power to enforce, by appropriate legislation, the provisions of this article.

Article XV *
(Amendment 15 - Rights of Citizens to Vote)

Section 1

The right of citizens of the United States to vote shall not be denied or abridged by the United States or by any State on account of race, color, or previous condition of servitude.

Section 2

The Congress shall have power to enforce this article by appropriate legislation.

* The Fifteenth Amendment was ratified February 3, 1870.

Article XVI *
(Amendment 16 - Income Tax)

The Congress shall have power to lay and collect taxes on incomes, from whatever source derived, without apportionment among the several States, and without regard to any census or enumeration.

* The Sixteenth Amendment was ratified February 3, 1913.

[Article XVII] *
(Amendment 17 - Popular Election of Senators)

The Senate of the United States shall be composed of two Senators from each State, elected by the people thereof, for six years; and each Senator shall have one vote. The electors in each State shall have the qualifications requisite for electors of the most numerous branch of the State legislatures.

When vacancies happen in the representation of any State in the Senate, the executive authority of such State shall issue writs of election to fill such vacancies: *Provided*, That the legislature of any State may empower the executive thereof to make temporary appointments until the people fill the vacancies by election as the legislature may direct.

This amendment shall not be so construed as to affect the election or term of any Senator chosen before it becomes valid as part of the Constitution.

* The Seventeenth Amendment was ratified April 8, 1913.

Article [XVIII] *
(Amendment 18 - Prohibition of Intoxicating Liquors)

[Section 1

After one year from the ratification of this article the manufacture, sale, or transportation of intoxicating liquors within, the importation thereof into, or the exportation thereof from the United States and all territory subject to the jurisdiction thereof for beverage purposes is hereby prohibited.

Section 2

The Congress and the several States shall have concurrent power to enforce this article by appropriate legislation.

Section 3

This article shall be inoperative unless it shall have been ratified as an amendment to the Constitution by the legislatures of the several States, as provided in the Constitution, within seven years from the date of the submission hereof to the States by the Congress.]

* The Eighteenth Amendment was ratified January 16, 1919. It was repealed by the Twenty-First Amendment, December 5, 1933.

Article [XIX] *
(Amendment 19 - Women's Suffrage Rights)

The right of citizens of the United States to vote shall not be denied or abridged by the United States or by any State on account of sex.

Congress shall have power to enforce this article by appropriate legislation.

* The nineteenth Amendment was ratified August 18, 1920.

Article [XX] *
(Amendment 20 - Terms of President, Vice President, Members of Congress: Presidential Vacancy)

Section 1

The terms of the President and Vice President shall end at noon on the 20th day of January, and the terms of Senators and Representatives at noon on the 3d day of January, of the years in which such terms would have ended if this article had not been ratified; and the terms of their successors shall then begin.

Section 2

The Congress shall assemble at least once in every year, and such meeting shall begin at noon on the 3d day of January, unless they shall by law appoint a different day. [affects 5]

Section 3

If, at the time fixed for the beginning of the term of the President, the President elect shall have died, the Vice

* The Twentieth Amendment was proposed by Congress on March 2, 1932. Ratification was completed on January 23, 1933, when the thirty-sixth State approved the amendment, there being 48 States in the Union..

President elect shall become President. If a President shall not have been chosen before the time fixed for the beginning of his term, or if the President elect shall have failed to qualify, then the Vice President elect shall act as President until a President shall have qualified; and the Congress may by law provide for the case wherein neither a President elect nor a Vice President elect shall have qualified, declaring who shall then act as President, or the manner in which one who is to act shall be selected, and such person shall act accordingly until a President or Vice President shall have qualified.

Section 4

The Congress may by law provide for the case of the death of any of the persons from whom the House of Representatives may choose a President whenever the right of choice shall have devolved upon them, and for the case of the death of any of the persons from whom the Senate may choose a Vice President whenever the right of choice shall have devolved upon them.

Section 5

Sections 1 and 2 shall take effect on the 15th day of October following the ratification of this article.

Section 6

This article shall be inoperative unless it shall have been ratified as an amendment to the Constitution by the legislatures of three-fourths of the several States within seven years from the date of its submission.

Article [XXI] *
(Amendment 21 - Repeal of Eighteenth Amendment)

Section 1

The eighteenth article of amendment to the Constitution of the United States is hereby repealed.

Section 2

The transportation or importation into any State, Territory, or possession of the United States for delivery or use therein of intoxicating liquors, in violation of the laws thereof, is hereby prohibited.

Section 3

This article shall be inoperative unless it shall have been ratified as an amendment to the Constitution by conventions in the several States, as provided in the Constitution, within seven years from the date of the submission hereof to the States by the Congress.

* The Twenty-First Amendment was ratified December 5, 1933.

Amendment XXII *
(Amendment 22 - Presidential Tenure)

Section 1

No person shall be elected to the office of the President more than twice, and no person who has held the office of President, or acted as President, for more than two years of a term to which some other person was elected President shall be elected to the office of the President more than once. But this article shall not apply to any person holding the office of President when this article was proposed by the Congress, and shall not prevent any person who may be holding the office of President, or acting as President, during the term within which this article becomes operative from holding the office of President or acting as President during the remainder of such term.

Section 2

This article shall be inoperative unless it shall have been ratified as an amendment to the Constitution by the legislatures of three-fourths of the several states within seven years from the date of its submission to the states by the Congress.

* The Twenty-Second Amendment was ratified February 27, 1951.

Amendment XXIII *
(Amendment 23 - Presidential Electors for the District of Columbia)

Section 1

The District constituting the seat of government of the United States shall appoint in such manner as the Congress may direct: A number of electors of President and Vice President equal to the whole number of Senators and Representatives in Congress to which the District would be entitled if it were a state, but in no event more than the least populous state; they shall be in addition to those appointed by the states, but they shall be considered, for the purposes of the election of President and Vice President, to be electors appointed by a state; and they shall meet in the District and perform such duties as provided by the twelfth article of amendment.

Section 2

The Congress shall have power to enforce this article by appropriate legislation.

* The Twenty-Third Amendment was ratified March 29, 1961.

Amendment XXIV *
(Amendment 24 - Abolition of the Poll Tax Qualification in Federal Elections)

Section 1

The right of citizens of the United States to vote in any primary or other election for President or Vice President, for electors for President or Vice President, or for Senator or Representative in Congress, shall not be denied or abridged by the United States or any state by reason of failure to pay any poll tax or other tax.

Section 2

The Congress shall have power to enforce this article by appropriate legislation.

* The Twenty-Fourth Amendment was ratified January 23, 1964.

Amendment XXV *
(Amendment 25 - Presidential Vacancy, Disability, and Inability)

Section 1

In case of the removal of the President from office or of his death or resignation, the Vice President shall become President.

Section 2

Whenever there is a vacancy in the office of the Vice President, the President shall nominate a Vice President who shall take office upon confirmation by a majority vote of both Houses of Congress.

Section 3

Whenever the President transmits to the President pro tempore of the Senate and the Speaker of the House of Representatives his written declaration that he is unable to discharge the powers and duties of his office, and until he transmits to them a written declaration to the contrary, such powers and duties shall be discharged by the Vice President as Acting President.

* The Twenty-Fifth Amendment was ratified February 23, 1967.

Section 4

Whenever the Vice President and a majority of either the principal officers of the executive departments or of such other body as Congress may by law provide, transmit to the President pro tempore of the Senate and the Speaker of the House of Representatives their written declaration that the President is unable to discharge the powers and duties of his office, the Vice President shall immediately assume the powers and duties of the office as Acting President.

Thereafter, when the President transmits to the President pro tempore of the Senate and the Speaker of the House of Representatives his written declaration that no inability exists, he shall resume the powers and duties of his office unless the Vice President and a majority of either the principal officers of the executive department or of such other body as Congress may by law provide, transmit within four days to the President pro tempore of the Senate and the Speaker of the House of Representatives their written declaration that the President is unable to discharge the powers and duties of his office. Thereupon Congress shall decide the issue, assembling within forty-eight hours for that purpose if not in session. If the Congress, within twenty-one days after receipt of the latter written declaration, or, if Congress is not in session, within twenty-one days after Congress is required to assemble, determines by two-thirds vote of both Houses that the President is unable to discharge the powers and duties of his office, the Vice President shall continue to discharge the same as Acting President; otherwise, the President shall resume the powers and duties of his office.

Amendment XXVI*
(Amendment 26 - Reduction of Voting Age Qualification)

Section 1

The right of citizens of the United States, who are 18 years of age or older, to vote, shall not be denied or abridged by the United States or any state on account of age.

Section 2

The Congress shall have the power to enforce this article by appropriate legislation.

* The Twenty-Sixth Amendment was ratified July 1, 1971.

Amendment XXVII *
(Amendment 27 - Congressional Pay Limitation)

No law varying the compensation for the services of the Senators and Representatives shall take effect until an election of Representatives shall have intervened.

* The Twenty-Seventh Amendment was ratified May 7, 1992. Originally proposed September 25, 1789.

Alexander Hamilton was an American statesman and one of the Founding Fathers of the United States. He was an influential interpreter and promoter of the U.S. Constitution, as well as the founder of the nation's financial system, the Federalist Party, the United States Coast Guard, and the *New York Post* newspaper.

Charles McCurdy "Mac" Mathias Jr. was a Republican member of the United States Senate, representing Maryland from 1969 to 1987.

The Story of the Constitution

by Former Senator Charles McC. Mathias, Jr.

William E. Gladstone may have been slightly misleading when he said that the United State Constitution was "the most remarkable work known to me in modern times to have been produced by the human intellect, at a single stroke."

There is no doubt that he intended a generous compliment nor any doubt that the Constitution is truly remarkable. The Constitutional Convention of the long, hot summer of 1787 might even be considered to have been that single stroke.

But Gladstone's statement does not reflect the experience of centuries in other societies and countries that has been woven into the Constitution. The historical and philosophical roots of the Constitution run very deep. We have been nourished by a long tradition of thought reaching back to the ancient Greeks.

The founders of our country were familiar with the writings of Plato, Aristotle, Cicero, Locke, and Montesquieu. It was their grasp of history and their knowledge of political thought that enabled them to transcend the moment and write a document which was, as the Preamble states, ". . . for ourselves and our posterity."

The principles of parliamentary practice were adapted from the British model. The doctrine of separation of powers was not merely expounded by Montesquieu; it was practiced in the Republic of Venice. The concept of independence of judges was respected in ancient Persia before the birth of Christ.

There were many strokes delivered by countless men and women who contributed to the evolution of political institutions. The intellectual creativity of the authors of the Constitution was not invention, but the application of historical lessons in a rational, coordinated, and successful system.

This remarkable work was the result of a series of events that culminated in Philadelphia. But the beginning hardly presaged the eventual end. From our vantage point the final product and its eventual ratification seemed inevitable. But the final success obscures the uncertainty that attended its development. In fact, the great Constitutional Convention did not begin as a constitutional convention at all. Rather, it was the out-growth of several earlier gatherings of much more modest aspirations.

Prior to 1776 there was no central colonial American government. Each colony had its own government that was answerable to the Crown. Within the framework of some general laws established by the mother country, each colony acted with autonomy from the others.

The signing of the Declaration of Independence furthered that autonomy by making the colonies separate and independent nations. But to fight a common war against a great power, more than an assertion of independence was needed. The Articles of Confederation provided a loose arrangement for cooperation among the sovereign states.

Under the Articles there was a legislature, a Congress with a single house, in which each state, regardless of its population, wielded only one vote. The sole executive power, the President of the Congress, merely presided over meetings, without any other independent authority. In fact, what little power the Articles delegated to the national legislature was virtually unenforceable. Congressional requisitions on the states for taxes or military supplies could be, and at times were, ignored. When peace finally arrived after eight years of war, the situation deteriorated. Without the unifying threat of British coercion and chastisement, rallying even minimal cooperation was difficult.

The promising beginning, symbolized by the bold words of freedom in the Declaration of Independence, seemed condemned to failure by the weaknesses in the Articles of Confederation. A hapless government floundered in the face of many serious challenges.

The British refused to withdraw from their outposts along the Great Lakes, despite their pledge to do so in the Treaty of Paris in 1783. The Spanish, who controlled vast tracts of land to the west of the thirteen states, closed the mouth of the Mississippi to commerce that was crucial to development of the states' own western territories. In addition, both Spain and England encouraged and armed the Indians to attack frontier settlements. Abroad, Barbary pirates preyed on American shipping, seizing cargo and holding American citizens for ransom. Unfortunately, the not yet united states of America could do little to protect themselves and their citizens. The Continental Army was disbanded after the war; and since American naval vessels no longer enjoyed British naval protection, overseas pirates encountered little resistance.

Added to these foreign problems were the domestic disputes among the independent states. One internal conflict in particular illustrates the point, and provided part of the impetus for what was to become the Constitutional Convention. In 1784, a dispute broke out between the watermen of Maryland and Virginia over the control of fishing in the Potomac River, which is wholly within Maryland, because its southern shore is the common boundary. The Virginians reacted to the curtailment of their freedom to fish in the Potomac by restricting the passage of Maryland ships through Cape Charles and Cape Henry, the gateway between the Chesapeake Bay and the Atlantic Ocean.

Thus Maryland commerce was blockaded and Virginia fishing suspended except on the onerous conditions each side laid down. The Articles of Confederation provided no method for resolving this dispute, and only George Washington's personal invitation to meet at Mt. Vernon produced a solution—the compact of 1785.

The dispute highlighted a major flaw in the organic law. So it was resolved to ask a more representative group to meet in Annapolis to consider some refinement of the Articles in the limited area of removing interference with interstate commerce. The meeting in Annapolis in September 1786, attended by delegates from only a few of the states, was unsuccessful and adjourned without agreement on the way to carry out this specific mandate. The delegates proposed to call a second session to meet in Philadelphia to complete the job.

There is every indication that the Philadelphia Convention had no authority to write a new constitution. Not even a broad revision of the Articles of Confederation was contemplated. As Patrick Henry exclaimed after the Constitutional Convention, during Virginia's debate over ratification, ". . . Who authorized them [the delegates at the Philadelphia Convention] to speak the language of 'We, the people' instead of 'We, the States?'. . . . The people gave them no power to use their name.... The federal convention ought to have amended the old system; for this purpose they were solely delegated. . . ."

But when the Constitutional Convention gathered, it conceived that it had supreme power to act in the name of the people, including the authority to define its own mandate. The need to amend was implied to include the right to replace. The result was so magnificent and successful that the Framers of the Constitution have been forgiven for actions that would have been ultra vires, beyond authority, for those who lacked their courage and their wisdom. As Alexis de Tocqueville observed some three and one-half decades later, "If ever there was a short moment when America did rise to that climax of glory where the proud imagination of her inhabitants would constantly like us to see her, it was at that supreme crisis when the national authority had in some sort abdicated its dominion."

Jefferson once referred to the fifty-five delegates who gathered in Philadelphia in 1787 as an assemblage of demigods. Indeed, most portrayals of the founders cast them with almost superhuman qualities. It is interesting to note the characteristics of the delegation that produced the Constitution. There were merchants from New England and planters from the South. Others were ministers, and over half were lawyers. Many were highly educated. The average age was 42, with Benjamin Franklin the oldest at 81 and Jonathan Dayton of New Jersey the youngest at 26. But most shared the experience of public service. More than two-thirds had served in the Continental Congress. Eighteen had been officers in the Continental Army and one had been a British officer before the Revolution. Some of the delegates had signed the Declaration of Independence and helped draft the Articles of Confederation. Some were governors, legislators, or judges in their home states.

Some prominent figures of the day were not present. Thomas Jefferson and John Adams represented the states as ministers to France and England respectively. Patrick Henry, suspicious of the prospect of greater federal authority, declined to serve as a delegate.

In the end thirty-eight delegates and one deputy delegate would put their names on the Constitution, to be sent to the states for ratification.

At the first official meeting in Independence Hall on May 25, George Washington was unanimously chosen as President. The choice was an obvious one. Only Benjamin Franklin came close to Washington in national and international acclaim. The proceedings of the

Convention were kept in strict secrecy to prevent the newspapers and the public from engaging in wild speculation. However, copious notes kept by James Madison provide our best insight into the debates.

At the outset, a conflict over state representation threatened to deadlock the Convention. As in the Congress established by the Articles of Confederation, each state, regardless of population, had one vote at the Convention. But the delegates disagreed about whether the less-populous states should be given equal representation in the national legislature. At the time of the Convention, over 40 percent of the population lived in three states: Pennsylvania, Massachusetts, and Virginia. Small states feared that under a proportional representation scheme, these three, allied with one or two less-populous states, could control the government. The intense loyalty most Americans felt for their own states sharpened the debate over the plan for a strengthened federal government.

Four plans on the issue of representation were submitted. The first proposal, referred to as the Virginia plan, was offered by James Madison. It provided for the supremacy of a bicameral legislature, a national executive, and a national system of courts. While representatives of one house of the legislature were to be popularly elected, delegates in the other house were to be nominated by the state legislatures but chosen by the first house. In this plan, representation in both houses was to be based on state population.

While Madison understood proportional state representation to be an important issue, it appears he underestimated the strength of opposition to his proposal. For Madison, the national government was to be an instrument of the people. Proportional representation ensured that citizens in large Virginia, for example, would count as much as the residents of tiny Connecticut.

Delegates from small states saw it differently. They feared that their interests would be constantly overrun by the desires of the more-populous states. Although big states resented the idea of equal congressional representation, they had lived with it from the start of the Articles of Confederation. Delegates from the small states, caught off guard by the submission of the Virginia plan, hastened to develop an alternative that preserved the status quo.

When the issue was first broached in late May, the proponents of proportional representation—through an alliance of big states and the deep South—had the votes to carry the proposal. However, to ram it through risked a walkout by the small-state delegates. The delegates from Delaware—the state that would eventually be the first to ratify the Constitution—claimed they were prohibited from accepting such a proposal and threatened to withdraw from the Convention proceedings.

A few days later a second plan was submitted by William Paterson of New Jersey. The New Jersey plan would have simply amended the Articles of Confederation. Congress would be given additional powers, and an executive would be chosen from the Congress, but all states would continue to have equal representation.

In a passionate defense of his plan, Paterson broadened the scope of the debate. Paterson reasoned that the states, being equally sovereign under the Articles of Confederation, could accept no proposal that diminished their authority. A government of proportional representation would enhance the power of the large states by giving them more votes in the national legislature. According to Paterson, the states' rights must be preserved, because the national government was to be responsible to the states and not directly to the people. Clearly the New Jersey plan called into question the premises of Madison's proposal—that the structure of the Articles of Confederation left the national government too weak to carry out its proper role. The Convention had reached a crossroads.

Delegates on each side of the issue refused to yield until a compromise offered by Roger Sherman of Connecticut saved the day. The compromise called for two houses of Congress with differing principles of suffrage. The House of Representatives would be popularly elected, with each state having representation based upon population. In the Senate, all states would be equally represented by members who would be chosen by the state legislatures.

Sherman's proposal was not immediately endorsed. Indeed, at one point when the debate became heated, Franklin offered his own plan, a complicated one that was delivered in a long, rambling speech. Franklin's proposal allowed time for tempers to cool. The "Great Compromise" was finally adopted. Delegates from large and small states united behind the plan.

The dispute over representation established an important precedent. As the summer wore on, other seemingly intractable disputes were resolved by balancing disparate interests. Northern commercial interests, for example, which strongly favored congressional authority to regulate commerce, ceded to the South the limitation that no duties would be levied on the export of their staple crops. In other instances as well, the delegates subordinated their parochial interests to the goal of unity.

What emerges in the final plan of the Convention is not only a balance of interests but a system of control on the increased authority given the new national government. The weaknesses of the Articles of Confederation would be corrected, but the new power would be checked by diffusing authority. Federal power would be circumscribed, leaving important functions to the states, and the separation of powers vested in three branches of government would provide carefully crafted checks and balances.

Article I of the Constitution articulates the range of congressional legislative authority. Many of the specific powers were taken from state constitutions and the Articles of Confederation.

One of the fundamental powers of any government is the power to raise revenue through taxation. Misuse of this authority, more than almost any other, has been responsible for changing history. The Magna Charta in 1215, the English Civil War that ousted Charles I, and the American Revolution itself were to a great extent outgrowths of disputes over taxation. The Founders were determined not to repeat this history. Since the legislature was to be more directly accountable than either of the other branches to the citizenry, the delegates at Philadelphia vested this authority in Congress, As Madison wrote in *Federalist* 48, "the legislative department alone has access to the pockets of the people,"

Congress was granted other crucial powers: to regulate interstate and foreign commerce, for example, and to declare war. But Congress' power was also limited: the privilege of the writ of habeas corpus could only be suspended if public safety required it, and no bill of attainder or *ex post facto* law could be enacted.

In addition, neither branch of Congress could legislate alone. Each house had a check on the actions of the other. The President's veto power provided a further restraint, which could be overcome only by a two-thirds majority vote of each house. However, the legislative branch was given a check on the President, for the chief executive can be removed from office by the Congress through impeachment, an historic British parliamentary procedure.

The experience of two centuries has demonstrated the wisdom of the Great Compromise and of the Framers' allocation of powers to the legislature. Today, the Senate is popularly elected. Congressional power has been circumscribed by the Bill of Rights, and has been expanded to provide for a federal income tax and for legislation to implement several other constitutional amendments. But in most other respects, Congress operates in accordance with the original constitutional plan.

Article I has proven sufficiently flexible to accommodate developments that its authors could not have anticipated. The power to regulate commerce, for example, has proven adaptable to the circumstances of a modern industrial nation as well as those of the agrarian economy of the late eighteenth century.

The development of political parties has also taken place within the framework of Article 1. It is difficult to imagine a Congress without parties; yet these institutions did not even exist in the Continental Congress or under the Articles of Confederation. Although the role of parties has changed over the course of history, at their best they provide another way to restrain authority and hold legislative majorities accountable to the people.

Article II of the Constitution establishes the executive branch. The debate over the executive provided another difficult problem for the delegates. While the Articles of Confederation demonstrated the need for a stronger executive, a war for independence from a king unresponsive to his subjects provided a telling counter-example. The delegates debated a plural executive, considered a term of life or seven years, before finally settling on a four-year renewable term. How to choose the President was also a perplexing question. In the two major plans offered—the New Jersey and the Virginia plans—the executive was to be elected by the legislature from among its members. However, it was feared that this would make the executive too subservient to Congress.

Once again a balanced compromise was reached. The President would be picked by an electoral college whose members were chosen by the people. The indirect, rather than popular, election of the President was favored as a limit on the influence of the larger states, and as a check on popular passions.

However, while the President would not be chosen directly by Congress, the delegates assumed that the House of Representatives and not the electoral college would often pick the President. Under Article II, a candidate for the presidency must receive a majority of the electoral college votes. If no candidate receives a majority, the House of Representatives must select the President, with each state delegation casting only one vote. The Founders believed that, except for Washington, no figure could command national acclaim, and therefore expected that the electoral college votes would usually be split among local candidates. With none receiving the necessary majority, the House would choose the President.

However, the development of political parties helped transcend sectional rivalries, with consequences unanticipated by the Framers. The adoption of the Twelfth Amendment, providing for separate balloting for President and Vice President, further changed the system. Only twice in our nation's history—in the 1801 election of Thomas Jefferson and the 1825 election of John Quincy Adams—has the House of Representatives chosen the President.

In addition to seeing that the laws are faithfully executed and acting as commander-in-chief of the armed forces, the President has some functions shared with the other branches. The power to veto is distinctly legislative, while the pardon power is judicial in nature. The power of appointment to office was divided between the President who nominates and the Senate which must confirm.

There is no doubt that the power of the modern presidency is far more extensive than the authors of Article I could have foreseen. The handful of clerks appointed by the first Presidents has grown into a federal establishment numbering millions of employees; and the selection of our chief executive has become a process of vital concern to people around the globe. But in recent years the Congress has reclaimed some of its restraint on the executive through general legislation, appropriations, and (in the case of the Senate) the advice and consent power. The development of judicial review has enabled the judicial branch to exercise a further check.

The Twenty-second Amendment limits the President to two terms, and the Twenty-fifth Amendment clarifies the circumstances under which the Vice President may succeed to the office. Apart from these minor adjustments, Article II has survived unchanged, establishing an executive authority that could meet the challenges imposed by a growing nation and yet remain responsive to the people.

Article III establishes the judicial branch and provides for federal judges with life tenure, appointed by the President with the advice and consent of the Senate. The Founders certainly appreciated the value of an independent judiciary, but never explicitly articulated its most important constitutional function—the power of judicial review.

As with so many fundamental notions, judicial review now seems an inevitable outgrowth of the balanced tripartite government. But the power of the judiciary to review legislative or executive action was not clearly asserted until 1805, in Chief Justice John Marshall's opinion in the case of *Marbury v. Madison*. Without this authority, the courts would be powerless to adjudicate conflicts between the Constitution and treaties, federal laws, and legislative and executive acts performed under its authority. In our century, the role of the courts in protecting the rights of minorities from the excesses of majority rule has become familiar. But in constitutional terms, the paramount value of judicial review is to protect the written Constitution from major alteration except as specified in the amendatory process established by Article V.

The issue of an amendatory process was debated at some length in Philadelphia. The Constitutional Convention did not set out to create a fixed, unchangeable system of government. Amendments to the Constitution would, with changing circumstances, be needed. The Philadelphia Convention set out to solve the practical problems that provided the impetus for its creation. As one delegate put it, a bit cynically, "Experience must be our only guide; reason may mislead us." But if the remarkable and experienced men of the Constitutional Convention felt free to go beyond their appointed bounds to completely change the fundamental charter, they were also well aware that such an experiment should not be lightly undertaken by their successors.

They were obviously concerned that the procedures for amending the Constitution be more flexible than those in the Articles of Confederation, which required the unanimous agreement of all the states. Once the Framers of the Constitution agreed that it should include a means for amendment, their subsequent debates centered around whether the power to amend should rest in the national or state legislatures, or both. They settled on both, and in No. 43 of *The Federalist* James Madison explains why:

> "The mode preferred by the convention seems to be stamped with every mark of propriety. It guards equally against the extreme facility which would render the Constitution too mutable; and the extreme difficulty which might perpetuate its discovered faults. It moreover equally enables the general and the state governments to originate the amendment of errors as they may be pointed out by the experience on one side or on the other."

The initial occasion for amending the Constitution followed its ratification by only a few months. From today's perspective, the Constitution would be incomplete without the first ten amendments. The Bill of Rights provides a symmetry to the Constitution, a fitting end to the debate surrounding ratification. As Madison wrote, "In framing a government which is to be administered by men over men, the difficulty lies in this: you must first enable the government to control the governed; and in the next place oblige it to control itself." Just as the Preamble of the Constitution establishes the authority granted the new government, deriving it from the people, the Bill of Rights restrains that authority, protecting important areas of individual autonomy.

The need for a bill of rights to complete the Constitution was by no means clear to the Framers. Five days before the end of the Constitutional Convention, the question of adding a bill of rights was raised by George Mason of Virginia, the principal author of the bill of rights in Virginia's state constitution of 1776. But the majority of the delegates opposed its incorporation at this time.

Some seemed to think that a bill of rights was not only unnecessary but potentially dangerous. Any important individual liberties that were omitted from a list of potential rights might be lost to the whim of a majority or abdicated to the government. Thus. the inclusion of a bill of rights might imply that the federal government was vested with power over individual liberty well beyond what is articulated in the Constitution's seven articles.

The Antifederalist opponents of ratification seized on the absence of a bill of rights as an argument for rejection of the Constitution by the states. For those who distrusted centralized government, the absence of specific restrictions on federal power over individual liberties epitomized what was wrong with the Constitution. This Antifederalist objection was difficult to discount. Even a moderate like Jefferson keenly felt that the lack of a bill of rights was the major liability in the charter. He wrote to Madison that "a bill of rights is what the people are entitled to against every government on earth, general or particular and what no just government should refuse, or rest on inference."

The debate over ratification of the Constitution was intense and the margin of victory small. Only the understanding that a bill of rights would be the first item on the national agenda of the new Congress brought favorable action from New York, Massachusetts, and Virginia. Indeed, these states appended a bill of rights to their ratification of the Constitution.

Even though the first Congress was hard at work building the new government-providing for a national revenue system, erecting the federal judiciary, and establishing the executive departments—Madison pressed the case for a bill of rights. Madison's determination arose from both philosophical conviction and pragmatic calculation. He believed that government, even if popularly supported, should be interdicted from infringing on personal liberty. But he also wanted to thwart the Antifederalist call for a second constitutional convention that could rewrite the fundamental charter.

Madison's initiative was successful. The first Congress sent twelve amendments to the states for ratification. Two amendments—one on proportional representation and the other on setting congressional salaries—were rejected. The other ten amendments became the Bill of Rights.

The terseness of the first ten amendments to the Constitution—none is longer than a single sentence—conclusively proves the proposition that a statement of principles need not be long to be powerful. The elaboration of these principles, and their application to the changing circumstances of two centuries, is the task to which the courts, and, in some cases, the Congress, have applied themselves.

Thomas Jefferson once observed that "the natural process of things is for liberty to yield and government to gain ground." If so, whenever Americans have sought to reverse this process and to preserve and expand the zones of freedom in our society, they have turned to the Bill of Rights for inspiration and sanction. Those struggles have taken forms of which the authors of the amendments could not have dreamed.

The Fourth Amendment, for example, was designed to prevent the abuse of power exemplified by the so-called writ of assistance. This was a general warrant that authorized officers of the Crown to search homes and property for smuggled goods, without specifying either the target or the object of the search. Colonial outrage over these writs helped fuel the fire of revolution.

The immediate goal of the drafters of the Fourth Amendment was to outlaw the hated general warrants. But when the electronic age spawned new threats against the privacy of Americans, the courts, after some false starts and wrong turns, came to recognize that the eighteenth-century prose of the Fourth Amendment embodies a principle that applies to a twentieth-century society with equal vigor. As Justice Louis Brandeis observed in his 1928 dissent in the case of Olmstead v. the United States, "the makers of the Constitution . . . conferred, as against the government, the right to be let alone—the most comprehensive of rights and the right most valued by civilized men." The Fourth Amendment prevents a modern American police force from an unwarranted telephone tap as surely as it prevented a Redcoat from rifling a Colonist's desk. And the development of yet more sophisticated methods of government intrusion means that the Fourth Amendment will have to meet similar challenges in the future.

A treasure trove of our national ideals is packed into the forty-five-word container of the First Amendment. Its authors meant to prevent the government from committing specific abuses: the establishment of a national church, for example, or the prior censorship of a newspaper. But the means they adopted for outlawing these excesses has also served to promote progress and harmony in a society whose hallmarks they could not have anticipated.

The First Amendment's guarantees of religious liberty are the major reason why, almost alone among peoples, Americans of hundreds of different religious creeds—many of which first developed in our own fertile soil—today live together in relative tranquility. The principles of freedom of speech and association that fence the government out of Americans' discussions of personal beliefs and political questions also restrain government interference with scientific research and communication. It is no coincidence that science and technology have flourished in a nation whose organic law incorporates the essential principle that Albert Einstein considered indispensable to all scientific progress: "freedom of expression in all realms of intellectual endeavor."

First Amendment values serve another purpose that suggests a key ingredient in the longevity and vitality of the Constitution itself. The authors of the First Amendment were well aware that freedom of expression and communication were crucial factors distinguishing democracy from dictatorship. As Madison himself observed: "Knowledge will forever govern ignorance; and a people who mean to be their own governors must arm themselves with the power which knowledge gives." The freedoms secured by the First Amendment are essential to our system of self-government. Paradoxically, the survival of the government established by the Constitution is due as much to the powers denied it as to those granted it by its fundamental charter.

Since the ratification of the Bill of Rights, more than ten-thousand amendments to the Constitution have been proposed; but only sixteen more amendments have run the procedural gauntlet established by Article V. Some have modified the structural provisions of the original Constitution, by providing for the popular election of senators (the Seventeenth Amendment), or by clarifying the procedures for election of the President (Twelfth Amendment) and for the succession to office of the Vice President (Twenty-fifth Amendment) for example. Others have extended the protections of the Bill of Rights (the Fourteenth Amendment) and provided fuller participation in the polity for excluded and powerless Americans (for example, the extension of the franchise to racial minorities, women, residents of the District of Columbia, and young adults, by the Fifteenth, Nineteenth, Twenty-third, and Twenty-sixth Amendments, respectively). Some amendments have expanded the powers of the federal government (for example, the Fourteenth Amendment, which extends the Bill of Rights to the states, and the Sixteenth Amendment, which authorizes a federal income tax); others have restrained federal power (such as the Eleventh Amendment, providing that the states generally cannot be sued in federal court without their consent).

But all the amendments have this in common: each tried to be a practical solution to a real problem with which the nation could not grapple within the existing constitutional framework. Some succeeded and others failed. But each sought to build on and perfect the system created in Philadelphia two hundred years ago.

Today, that system continues to perform the tasks for which it was designed. It was designed to prevent tyranny, and so it disperses power among the branches and levels of government rather than concentrating power to promote efficiency. It was designed to focus government power on its legitimate objectives; and so government remains fenced out of our houses of worship, our newsrooms, and the private precincts of our families. It was designed to enfranchise the people; and so the electoral process opens to an ever-expanding circle of Americans entitled to exercise their sovereignty.

* * *

The guide to the burning constitutional debates of our nation's third century will not be found in the text of the Constitution itself. The document cannot tell us which of its provisions will function peacefully through the next hundred years and which will erupt into contention and dispute. The Constitution's future will follow the course established by the challenges our society must confront in the next century.

Above all, the Constitution is a practical document, drawn up by practical men facing practical problems. Those men applied to the task a thorough familiarity with history, a subtle understanding of human nature, and an evident respect for the English language. But their handiwork has persisted and endured, not because of its theoretical coherence, or the elegant symmetry of the federal structure it created, or its graceful prose, but because it has worked.

The Constitution succeeded in solving the pressing problems the young nation faced in 1787. With necessary amendments, it has continued to provide a means for a nation grown ever more powerful, prosperous, and complex to grapple with the problems presented to it by a dangerous and interdependent world.

Its future will depend on the ability of a self-governing nation of free men and women to find within this rich and living charter the means to confront the challenges of the centuries ahead.

Thomas Phillip "Tip" O'Neill Jr., was an American politician who served as the 47th Speaker of the United States House of Representatives from 1977 to 1987, representing northern Boston, Massachusetts, as a Democrat from 1953 to 1987. Shown here with President Reagan.

What the Constitution Means to Us Today

(written in 1986)

by The Honorable Thomas P. "Tip" O'Neill
Former Speaker of the House of Representatives

If you asked ten people on the street if they thought the United States Constitution was "old" or "young" when compared with the constitutions of other countries, I would bet that most people would say ours is young. We Americans see ourselves as part of the "New World," which our ancestors came to from all parts of the "Old World." The truth, however, is that we have the oldest written constitution in continuous operation in the world. We may be a young nation when compared to some of the ancient kingdoms and empires of the world, but we are the oldest representative democracy on the planet. About two-thirds of the world's governments have constitutions drafted since 1970. Ours dates back to 1787.

The Framers of the Constitution were a remarkable group of men who were experienced in government and who knew their history. They created a government that had a powerful new idea. They said the power of government comes from the people themselves and not from a king. They turned the world of the eighteenth century, a world dominated by kings, emperors, and autocrats, on its head when they designed a constitution that began "We the People."

The House of Representatives, where I have had the honor of serving for thirty-four years, the last ten years as Speaker, is the part of government that is closest to the people. It is the first branch of government described in Article I of the Constitution. It is the part of government that has to face the regular scrutiny of the voters every two years, and for the first 124 years under the Constitution it was the only popularly elected house of the Congress, since senators were elected by state legislatures until the seventeenth Amendment provided for their direct election. The House, as the part of government closest to the people, is responsible for introducing all revenue bills.

The Framers of the Constitution envisioned that the House and the Senate would play an extremely important role in this three-part government. They assumed, for example, that most of the time the House would elect the President of the United States (Article II, Section 1, and the Twelfth Amendment). But the Framers failed to foresee the development of the two-party system that has become a hallmark of American politics. As a result, the House has been called upon only twice, after the elections in 1800 and in 1824, to elect the President. It is clear that the Framers expected the three branches of the federal government to be able to check excess power from one branch or the other. The story of American political history can be told in large part by the drama of the tug of war between the three branches as they exercised the powers given to them in the Constitution. This system of checks and balances is one of the truly ingenious parts of the Constitution.

When you read in your newspapers or see on television where the House or the Senate are differing with the President on some issue, you should be able to look at that clash of ideas on several levels. Depending on the issue, it may be party politics that will explain the disagreement, or it may be a more fundamental constitutional issue. Under our Constitution it is not the duty of the House or the Senate to accede to the wishes of the President just because the President occupies the Oval Office. The strength of our government over two hundred years has come from the ability of those in office to live up to the principles of the Constitution to check the excessive power of anyone branch of the government. The Constitution spells out the rules under which the three branches relate to one another. Following these rules is not always an easy task. The system of checks and balances does not always lead to the highest rate of efficiency in government. But how shall we measure efficiency? Shall we define efficiency only by budgets and solutions to immediate problems, or shall we take a larger view that real efficiency means providing a stable government that offers expanded opportunities to improve representative democracy and individual freedom? Dictatorships are efficient, but that's not the kind of efficiency in government that Americans want.

One of the stories often told about how the Framers viewed the main difference between the House and the Senate is an exchange that supposedly took place between Thomas Jefferson and George Washington. The conversation may never have taken place exactly as it has been passed down, and I'm not sure it expressed Washington's view of the House, but its enduring value is in the principle it explains. Jefferson, who was in France when the Constitution was drafted, was surprised to see that the Congress had a House and a Senate rather than a unicameral (one house) legislature. He asked Washington why this was so. Washington supposedly asked Jefferson why he poured his tea in his saucer before drinking it. "To cool it," replied Jefferson. "Just so," Washington explained, "we pour House legislation into the senatorial saucer to cool it." The House, as the peoples' body, supposedly would be more passionate than the cool and detached Senate. This story helps explain some of the checks built into the Constitution to ensure that legislation was based on deliberation, not on the emotion of the moment. But, over two hundred years, there have been some twists in it. In many cases it is the House that has had to cool the passions of the Senate. As the House has grown in size, it has developed stricter rules of procedure than has the Senate, which still has the luxury of unlimited debate. But in either case the system of checks and balances in our two-house legislature has worked pretty well.

* * *

The country and the world have changed tremendously in the [over] two hundred years since the Constitution was drafted. We have grown from a collection of thirteen relatively weak states with a population of about 4 million to one of the world's superpowers with a population of 243 million stretching from the Atlantic to the Pacific, and out to Hawaii and up to Alaska. In the time the Constitution has been in effect we have gone from horse power to nuclear power. We have explored this planet and extended our reach to the stars. We have suffered economic hardships, we have fought major wars on our own soil and overseas, and we have also prospered as no other nation on earth. The bedrock of our success has been the enduring Constitution and our ability and desire to uphold and defend it and the remarkable representative democracy that it has fostered.

Robert Joseph Dole is a retired American politician and attorney who represented Kansas in the U.S House of Representatives from 1961 to 1969 and in the U.S. Senate from 1969 to 1996, serving as the Republican Leader of the United States Senate from 1985 until 1996.

The Constitution and the Congress

by Former Senator Robert Dole

The first thing one notices about our Constitution is how much attention it devotes to the legislative branch of the federal government. The first and longest article created the Senate and House, established their officers and qualifications for election, and defined their powers. This extensive treatment is not surprising when we consider that prior to the Constitution our national government consisted of only a legislature—and a single-body legislature at that. The genius of the Constitution of 1787 was its division of the government into separate legislative, executive, and judicial branches, with a healthy system of checks and balances between them. In this system, the Senate received exclusive authority to ratify treaties, confirm appointments, and try impeachments. We share considerable other legislative power and responsibility with the House of Representatives, and we contend with the other branches for a share of the Constitution's "implied powers."

United States senators know full well from their daily experiences that the Constitution is not just a venerable parchment to be held up for display, but is the basic contract under whose terms we pledge to make this government work. Sometimes we may feel frustrated with its checks and complain about its imbalances. We may bemoan its inefficiencies and argue about its implications. But then we remember that the Constitution has stood the test of over two hundred years, that it has enabled this nation to grow and develop beyond the grandest dreams of its Framers, and that it has preserved and protected our basic rights and liberties. . . .

Chronology of the Constitution

SEPT. 11-14. 1786: The Annapolis Convention is held. On the final day, representatives adopt a resolution calling for a constitutional convention in Philadelphia the following spring, to address various concerns of the states about the Articles of Confederation.

FEB. 4. 1787: A local militia is able to suppress Shays' Rebellion, an uprising of destitute farmers in Massachusetts, but the revolt underscores the weakness of the present federal government.

MAY 25. 1787: The Constitutional Convention opens as a quorum of delegates from seven states convenes in Philadelphia, to discuss revising the Articles of Confederation. Soon, representatives from 12 of the 13 states are in attendance. Rhode Island alone will not join the Convention.

MAY 29. 1787: Edmund Randolph proposes the Virginia Plan. He would abandon the present constitution and form a new organization of government, including a bicameral legislature with proportional representation of the states in both chambers, a president chosen by the legislature, a judiciary branch, and a council comprised of the executive and the judiciary branch with a veto over legislative enactments.

JUNE 15. 1787: The New Jersey Plan is proposed by William Paterson, who views the Virginia Plan as disadvantageous to smaller states. His plan would only modify the Articles of Confederation, giving Congress the power to tax and to regulate foreign and interstate commerce, and establishing a plural executive (without veto power) and a supreme court.

JUNE 19. 1787: The Constitutional Convention votes to strike the Articles of Confederation, choosing instead to form a new national government.

JUNE 21. 1787: The Convention adopts a two-year term for representatives.

JUNE 26. 1787: The Convention adopts a six-year term for senators.

JULY 12. 1787: The Convention adopts the first part of Roger Sherman's Connecticut Compromise, making representation in the lower house proportional to a state's population.

JULY 16. 1787: The Convention adopts the second part of the Connecticut Compromise, allowing each state to be represented equally in the upper chamber.

AUG. 6. 1787: The initial draft of the Constitution, with 23 articles, is submitted to the floor, and the Great Debate begins. It will last until September 10.

AUG. 16. 1787: The Convention grants Congress the right to regulate foreign commerce and interstate trade.

SEPT. 6. 1787: The Convention adopts a four-year term for the president.

SEPT. 12. 1787: The final draft of the Constitution, written primarily by Gouverneur Morris of New York, is submitted to the floor for evaluation.

SEPT. 17. 1787: The Constitution is approved by all 12 states' delegations, and is signed by 39 of the 42 delegates present. The Convention formally adjourns.

SEPT. 28. 1787: The Congress of the Confederation resolves to submit the Constitution to the states for ratification. The document is to take effect after nine of the 13 states approve it.

OCT. 27. 1787: The first "Federalist" paper appears in New York City newspapers. It is one of 85, written by Alexander Hamilton, James Madison, and John Jay, that argue in favor of adoption of the Constitution and a strong centralized national government.

DEC. 7. 1787: Delaware is the first state to ratify the Constitution.

DEC. 12. 1787: Pennsylvania becomes the second state to ratify the Constitution.

DEC. 18. 1787: New Jersey becomes the third state to ratify the Constitution.

JAN. 2. 1788: Georgia becomes the fourth state to ratify the Constitution.

JAN. 9. 1788: Connecticut becomes the fifth state to ratify the Constitution.

FEB. 6. 1788: Massachusetts becomes the sixth state to ratify the Constitution, but only after Federalists propose nine amendments, including one which would reserve to the states all powers not "expressly delegated" to the federal government by the Constitution.

APRIL 28. 1788: Maryland becomes the seventh state to ratify the Constitution.

MAY 23. 1788: South Carolina becomes the eighth state to ratify the Constitution.

JUNE 21. 1788: The Constitution becomes official when New Hampshire ratifies it, the ninth state to do so.

JUNE 25. 1788: Virginia becomes the tenth state to ratify the Constitution, but recommends a bill of rights for American citizens.

JULY 2. 1788: The Congress of the Confederation announces that the Constitution has been ratified by the requisite number of states.

JULY 26. 1788: New York becomes the 11th state to ratify the Constitution.

SEPT. 13. 1788: New York City is selected as the site of the new government.

DEC. 23. 1788: Maryland cedes ten square miles of land to Congress, for a new federal city.

FEB. 4. 1789: Presidential electors select George Washington as the first President of the new government, and John Adams as the Vice President. States elect representatives and senators for the new U.S. Congress.

MARCH 4. 1789: The first U.S. Congress convenes in New York City.

APRIL 1. 1789: The House of Representatives achieves a quorum, and Frederick A. Muhlenberg of Pennsylvania is elected the first Speaker of the House.

APRIL 6. 1789: The Senate achieves a quorum, and John Langdon of New Hampshire is chosen to be temporary presiding officer.

APRIL 30. 1789: George Washington is inaugurated as the first President of the United States. He is sworn in by Robert Livingston, Chancellor of the State of New York.

JULY 27. 1789: Congress establishes a Department of Foreign Affairs (later renamed Department of State).

AUG. 7. 1789: Congress establishes a War Department.

SEPT. 2. 1789: Congress establishes a Treasury Department.

SEPT. 22. 1789: Congress establishes the position of Postmaster General.

SEPT. 24. 1789: Congress establishes a Supreme Court, thirteen district courts, three circuit courts, and the position of Attorney General.

SEPT. 25. 1789: Congress submits amendments to the Constitution to the states for ratification, known as the Bill of Rights. In order for the amendments to take effect, three-fourths of the states must ratify them.

SEPT. 26. 1789: John Jay is appointed the first Chief Justice of the United States, and Edmund Randolph is the first Attorney General.

NOV. 20. 1789: New Jersey ratifies the Bill of Rights of the amendments submitted to the states by Congress in September, the first state to do so.

NOV. 21. 1789: North Carolina becomes the 12th state to ratify the Constitution, after Congress proposes a Bill of Rights.

DEC. 19. 1789: Maryland becomes the second state to ratify the Bill of Rights.

DEC. 22. 1789: North Carolina becomes the third state to ratify the Bill of Rights.

JAN. 25. 1790: New Hampshire becomes the fourth state to ratify the Bill of Rights.

JAN. 28. 1790: Delaware becomes the fifth state to ratify the Bill of Rights.

FEB. 27. 1790: New York becomes the sixth state to ratify the Bill of Rights.

MARCH 10. 1790: Pennsylvania becomes the seventh state to ratify the Bill of Rights.

MAY 29. 1790: Rhode Island ratifies the Constitution, the last of the original states to do so.

JUNE 7. 1790: Rhode Island becomes the eighth state to ratify the Bill of Rights.

JULY 16. 1790: George Washington signs legislation selecting the District of Columbia as the permanent national capital, to be occupied in 1800.

DEC. 6. 1790: Philadelphia becomes the temporary site of the federal government.

JAN. 10. 1791: Though not yet a state, Vermont ratifies the Constitution.

MARCH 4. 1791: Vermont is admitted into the Union as the fourteenth state.

NOV. 3. 1791: Vermont ratifies the Bill of Rights.

DEC. 15. 1791: Virginia ratifies the Bill of Rights, and the amendments become part of the United States Constitution.

For special sales or editions,
please contact the publisher at bricktower@aol.com

Available to the trade from Ingram Content,
www.IngramContent.com

www.ingramcontent.com/pod-product-compliance
Lightning Source LLC
Chambersburg PA
CBHW060048210326
41520CB00009B/1304

9781883283001